Truman Capote's
In Cold Blood:

BOOKMARKED

JUSTIN ST. GERMAIN

PUBLISHING
New York, NY

Printed in the United States of America.
10 9 8 7 6 5 4 3 2 1

Ig Publishing
Box 2547
New York, NY 10163

www.igpub.com

ISBN: 978-1-63246-123-0

For Bonnie

CONTENTS

PART I

The Documentary Impulse

I first read Truman Capote's *In Cold Blood* fourteen years ago, because I had to. It was required reading for English 566: The Documentary Impulse, a class that met Tuesday nights on the fourth floor of Modern Languages, a brick edifice on the University of Arizona campus typical of humanities buildings at state universities: dour, desolate, clinging to dignity with a fatalistic charm. Modern Languages had a brutalist vibe, was full of asbestos, and somehow, in five decades of housing abbreviation-happy academics, had never been given a nickname, although we sometimes said its full name in silly accents.

I had inhabited Modern Languages for five years by then, through my undergraduate English major and my first year of grad school. Those scuffed linoleum halls felt like my second home, probably because they had so much in common with my first one, Tombstone, the Old West tourist town seventy miles away where I'd grown up. Both were moribund and lovable, haunted by the ghosts of their own relevance, among other things: English majors told tales of an apparition in the Modern Languages basement, some woman who'd been murdered long ago. Isn't that always the story?

I was twenty-four at the time, halfway through a master's of fine arts program in fiction writing. It's hard to remember who I was then, and harder still to write truthfully about a person who no longer exists. The surviving evidence suggests I wasn't doing especially well in graduate school, which was not surprising. I had never been a good student. As a child, I attended poor and penal public schools, on Army bases and in the rural borderlands of Arizona, a state constantly competing with its neighbor, New Mexico, for the title of the worst education system in America. I focused mostly on sports and girls and trouble, graduated with a middling GPA, and wound up at community college—three of them, in fact—where I failed half of my classes before matriculating at the University of Arizona, the only real college that accepted me, because I was in-state, and they pretty much had to. It was also the only four-year university I applied to, and the only one I'd ever seen.

My family weren't college people. We were what college people like to call working class or first-generation, or, behind closed doors, rednecks or white trash. People in my family joined the military after high school—my parents met on an Army base—and later worked blue-collar jobs, got married, had kids, got divorced, nursed habits, died young. The only person I knew who went to college was my older brother, who also went to the University of Arizona, which was the main reason I applied there. At the time, U of A was best known for its powerhouse basketball program and its yearly ranking on *Playboy*'s list of the best party schools in America.

Four years and a few stints of academic probation later, I graduated with a degree in English. My plan had been to move back to Tombstone and teach high school, but during a fiction class I took as an elective, the professor told me I could probably be a writer, if I wanted to.[1] He suggested I apply to MFA programs, wrote me a letter of recommendation, and probably got me into Arizona's, the only one that accepted me. They even offered me a assistantship that paid me to teach freshman writing while I went to school, which meant that I could afford to go.

And so, in the fall of 2005, my wayward education led me to a desk near the back of Modern Languages 428, a too-bright institutional room where I would spend the next sixteen Tuesday nights learning about The Documentary

---

1. He said it with a solemn resignation I wouldn't understand until much later.

Impulse. I didn't know what that meant, and didn't care much. I took the class because it was taught by Dr. Bertsch, a young, ironical, sort of punk-rock literature professor I knew from undergrad. Dr. Bertsch had recently been profiled in *The Believer*,[2] which made him something of a celebrity around Modern Languages, and certainly the most famous person I'd ever met. The article describes him like so:

> He's a big, thoughtful, friendly fellow with a clipped goatee, an earring, and a sloping bald forehead flanked by unruly brown hair. He has pointy incisors and a heavy Germanic brow; they conspire with his overwhelming generosity and goofy grin to make him seem a cross between Santa Claus and Faust.[3]

All of which is accurate, although in a selective sense. The article's portrayal reflected the writer's agenda, and that of the magazine itself, a sort of arch detachment typical of American nonfiction at the time. It leaves out Dr. Bertsch's defining feature—a furtive, absurd brilliance, an omission I resented. I had a dismaying tendency to dismiss other people's writing, especially when it appeared in the places I wanted to be published, and I wrote the article off as

2. Lewis-Kraus, Gideon. "In the Penthouse of the Ivory Tower." July 1, 2004. https://believermag.com/in-the-penthouse-of-the-ivory-tower.
3. Ibid.

another in a long line of David Foster Wallace imitations.[4] (I didn't know it at the time, but the tradition of the jaunty, condescending travelogue went back much further than that: Capote had helped popularize it fifty years earlier, with *The Muses Are Heard*, his account of a trip to Soviet Russia.) Later, Dr. Bertsch would tell me that the article's author had been uncomfortable with the responsibility of portraying him, and had consulted with him to make the portrayal a collaborative effort, a selective self they could both live with.

Dr. Bertsch had taught my first college English course, an American lit survey I should have failed; I rarely attended and handed in all the essays late, but my mother died in the middle of that semester, so he gave me a gentleman's C. Later, in an attempt to make amends, I took his literary analysis course, but missed a lot of class again, got a B, and generally failed to make an impression. Dr. Bertsch knew who I was, but I doubt he was happy to see me on the roster of a challenging graduate class.

Despite my dismal performance in his classes, Dr. Bertsch was my favorite professor. He had, in his oblique and mysterious way, shaped my sense of what literature meant. I'd spent my whole childhood reading, in the scattershot way of bookish kids in TV families: I read whatever was

---

4. I had a similarly dismaying tendency to compare everything to David Foster Wallace, who had gone to Arizona in the 1980s, and was sort of a legend around Modern Languages at the time.

around, whether that meant pulp Westerns or my stepdad's gun magazines or paperbacks from the Wal-mart in the next town over. And I read a lot, which made me an oddball in a place that wasn't big on book learning. My high school English classes mostly watched movies, *Macbeth* and *Romeo and Juliet*. Only the real nerds read recreationally.

Once I got to college and declared an English major, I got my first glimpse of the literary universe. I'd like to say it was some great revelation, but I spent most of my time in literature classes listening to old white guys talk about dead ones. Dr. Bertsch was different. He assigned books by women and writers of color; his American lit classes were my first exposure to Joan Didion, James Baldwin, Willa Cather.[5] In a textbook from his class, I read the speech Cochise, the Chiricahua Apache chief, gave on the occasion of his surrender; it was the first I'd heard of it, even though I grew up in a county named after him. That's how Dr. Bertsch's classes felt, like the things we read were chosen just for me. They made me want to be a book person, made me believe maybe I could. A year before The Documentary Impulse, when I'd found myself a newly minted teaching assistant, on the first floor of Modern Languages, down there with the ghosts, standing in front of my first class—a responsibility I

---

5. Cather was one of Capote's favorite writers; late in her life, they briefly met, an occasion he describes in one of his final essays, "Nocturnal Turnings."

was in no way prepared for—I'd tried to channel Dr. Bertsch. I would continue to do so for the rest of my teaching career.

It was harder than I expected to imitate him. Dr. Bertsch was the strangest teacher I had ever seen. He taught genre fiction and TV commercials alongside continental theory; he used baseball analogies to explain critical paradigms in class; he scrawled unfamiliar terms on the board in slanted, slightly deranged capitals, with arrows running back and forth between them, signifying something; he did drawings, too, circles and triangles and the occasional stick man. I never fully understood anything he said, but damn, did I want to. He once called a Pynchon novel[6] a code without a key, a line I'll never forget. Most of what I remember from college are things Dr. Bertsch said in class. I took the Documentary Impulse because I knew by then that I could learn from him, and I was trying to show my respect and admiration for him the only way I knew how, through loyalty. This time around, I wanted to impress him.

It didn't shape up to be easy. On the first day, when most of my other professors read the syllabus out loud and let us go early, we watched *Night and Fog*, a French documentary about the Holocaust. It was an interesting choice of film to show in our first class, at eight at night, in a haunted building, and it set a tone for the quarter. The next week, we were scheduled

---

6. *The Crying of Lot 49*, which he called one of his favorite novels. It soon became one of mine.

to discuss natural disasters and watch home movies of the catastrophic Indian Ocean tsunami the year before; the night the class met, Hurricane Katrina was ravaging New Orleans on the national news, a disaster documentary broadcast live to our classroom. As we got deeper into the class, deeper into fall, the room's two windows winked out earlier, until we were meeting entirely in the dark. Two days after the fourth anniversary of September 11th, we watched experimental documentaries about the attacks, and a few of my classmates who were more typical of humanities graduate students— wealthy and sheltered—started a class conversation about the lack of images from the Iraq War in what they insisted on calling *our* culture. I kept my mouth shut, for once, then went home and logged onto my still-new Facebook account, where I saw photos of my high school classmates wearing body armor, holding rifles, slouching against ancient masonry.

The first unit of the Documentary Impulse was about the relationship between documentary and trauma; we were working our way up to *In Cold Blood*. I'd bought the book the first week of class, at a since-closed independent bookstore Dr. Bertsch flouted university policy to support. It had been sitting ever since on the kitchen counter of my apartment, its cover beckoning darkly. My copy, which I still have— marked-up, yellowed, its spine held together with packing tape—is the first Vintage International edition, published in 1994, a paperback with two photos portmanteaued on its cover. The bottom one, black and white and vignetted at the edges, shows a street in Holcomb, Kansas, commanded by a white water tower. At the top edge of the page, a pair of human eyes stare out from a green rectangle, the eyes of a killer, although I didn't know that yet. I'd heard of the book before, but only knew it was about a murder in the Midwest. Most of the other texts we read were labors, and despite my best efforts to impress Dr. Bertsch—who, with his permission, I hesitantly began to address as Charlie—I didn't finish half of the readings. But I admit, I was intrigued by *In Cold Blood*. I'd been waiting a long time to read it; I just didn't know it yet.

•

Might as well get it out of the way: my mother was murdered. My stepdad shot her. It happened in the middle of the first class I took of Charlie's. The fourth anniversary came a month into the Documentary Impulse. Her death wasn't something I acknowledged. In the place I came from, remote and poor, steeped in the laconic myths of the West, people didn't discuss their grief; like all sufferings, it was a private shame to be endured. My mother's murder made me a morbid celebrity in my hometown, which was why I applied to MFA programs instead of moving back to teach high school like I'd planned. I wasn't cut out for grad school, but it was the only place where nobody knew me as the guy whose mom got murdered, and I loved that feeling so much it kept me enrolled. The only person in my new world who knew was Charlie.

I didn't write about my mother's death, either. I wrote short stories set in my hometown, about people like me who weren't actually me, as I often found myself insisting. My stories didn't go over well with my peers, and I couldn't tell if the writing sucked or if my readers didn't understand the world I was writing about; it didn't occur to me for some time that the answer might be both. My professors said to write what you know, so I wrote about kids dying in car wrecks, domestic violence, wildfires. Most of the other graduate students came from wealth; they claimed not to, of course, but you could tell by what they wrote about: vacations, their parents' divorces, the lives of Brooklynites with no jobs. I'd never been to Brooklyn, couldn't find it on a map, and I felt lost, like maybe I'd made another one of those bad decisions people were always talking about people like me making. I'd worked at the campus newspaper in college, and had almost gone into journalism; the local paper had offered me a part-time job, which I turned down to go to grad school. I was starting to regret that decision, and to think maybe I should've been a reporter: the few short stories I wrote that were any good were all basically true, anyway. I was failing at writing fiction, but I still believed all that grandiose bullshit about deeper truths, so I never considered nonfiction. Sure, all my stories were about guys with dead mothers, but I refused to fictionalize her death, and what else was I going to do, write a memoir?

Even if I wanted to, it seemed wrong to write about another person's murder. My mother's death was holy and ineffable. It had become one of those words people threw around in grad school, the ones I didn't understand: a metanarrative, an ouroboros. I refused to be defined by it, refused even to acknowledge it. Her murder wasn't mine to tell: as I often told myself, it didn't actually happen to me. Writing about it was out of the question. Instead I just thought about it all the time.

The day after the anniversary of her murder, we talked in Charlie's class about the ethics of representation. We watched clips of early experimental documentaries—Walter Ruttman's *Berlin, Symphony of a Great City*; Dziga Vertov's *Man With a Movie Camera*—and discussed theory texts about different documentary modes, how they portray the people in them, and what that means. There was a lot of talk about the sign/referent relationship, eyes and arrows and stick figures drawn on the board, terms like aesthetics and poetics, modalities of desire, praxis. I was compelled, drawn to the material by some subconscious sense of its significance, but not even Charlie's explanations and diagrams could make me understand what it all meant, and I wasn't about to ask questions and reveal my ignorance. The concepts flitted through my mind and faded. They wouldn't start to stick until a few weeks later, when we read *In Cold Blood*.

•

On November 15, 1959, four members of the Clutter family—Herbert, Bonnie, Nancy, and Kenyon—were murdered in their home at the edge of Holcomb, a remote farm town in western Kansas. Soon after the murders, Truman Capote went to Kansas to write about them. The result was *In Cold Blood*, a classic still relevant half a century later; in class, Charlie called it probably the most famous American work of nonfiction.

I remember disliking the book the first time I read it, but the evidence says otherwise. Charlie made us write online journals, or "blogs"; his syllabus put the words in quotes, because they were still necessary then. Blogging had existed for a decade, in various forms, but was ascendant at the time. Services like LiveJournal and Blogger had recently perfected software that allowed anyone to post content online; that content was usually drawn from the author's real lives, and blogs were popular in part because of their perceived honesty. YouTube was in its infancy, so video hadn't taken over yet, and social media in its contemporary form—beset by length restrictions, partisan hatred, brand promotion, and privacy concerns—didn't yet exist.[7] The semester I took Charlie's class may have been the peak of blogs. Nonfiction had gone democratic.

Charlie had adopted blogging early, as a teaching tool and an experiment in the online persona. He'd been keeping his own personal LiveJournal as long as I'd known him. It was professional in tone—he understood as early as anyone the ramifications of an online self—and he posted about teaching and the academic life, but also about his daughter, the San Francisco Giants, archival materials. I learned as much from his online persona as I did from his classroom presence: books to read, music to hear, and—most relevantly, although I didn't know it at the time—how to think and write like a college professor. Charlie's LiveJournal profile currently lists 135 friends,[8] so he may not have been the internet celebrity we thought he was, but his students, myself included, were widely and sheepishly devoted to his blog. The self he put online was mediated, of course, but it *seemed* so authentic: a real, smart person, on the internet.

He had us sign up for LiveJournals of our own. Mine is, dismayingly, still online. It's hard to read: I chose black text on a gray background, for some reason, and the person who

---

7. The next year, Twitter launched as a "microblogging" service, and Facebook co-opted blogging in the form of status updates, which probably spelled the end of the longform blogging boom, although many still exist.
8. Many others must have been lost to time and entropy.

wrote it is a long-dead version of me. But not really: the person on the page was a persona, one I was then inventing. The Documentary Impulse had worked on my writerly mind like a key in a lock, and tumblers were clicking into place: the sign/referent relationship, modes of representation, how to put a human on a page. Even back then, I knew the person I was in text was not the person I was in life. He was the sign, and I was the referent, or something like that. I didn't yet understand how that relationship would unfold over time, that the person I actually was then would disappear, fade into a ghost. Only the false self survives, the persona, the narrator, and he would change over the years into this person. But this is an act, too, and by the time you read these words, they'll be all that's left of who I was when I typed them.

Charlie wanted us to write about the course texts on our blogs, and comment on each other's posts; they were intended to be an extension of the classroom, a forum for further discussion. I was never good with directions: I wrote about whatever came to mind, including a late-night entry about Elliott Smith bootlegs that has nothing to do with the course. Surprisingly, I didn't have much to say about *In Cold Blood* the first time I read it. When I was halfway through reading the book, I posted briefly about the movie *Capote*, which had just been released at the time, but wasn't playing yet in Tucson. Only one paragraph discusses my response to the book itself, which I seem to have liked. It focuses on

Capote's use of a third-person omniscient point of view, a mode that can access the thoughts of multiple characters:

> It's a great book on a lot of levels, but perhaps most interesting to me in terms of the craft choices he makes. I just read a passage in which he gives a scene in Dick's point of view, then renders the exact same scene in Perry's. I'm not sure I've ever seen that before.

I was thinking about portrayal and representation, but only in the craft terms I learned in my fiction workshops. Like a lot of novice nonfiction writers—Capote included—I saw the genre through the lens of fiction, a critical framework I would later come to see as a deficient way to think about documentary forms. I knew there was something strange happening in Capote's book, and point of view was part of it, but I couldn't put my finger on what my problem was, and I probably didn't try that hard. It would be convenient for the purposes of this book to privilege my memory, that fiction machine, and say that I was obsessed with *In Cold Blood* the first time I read it. The historical record suggests otherwise: I promised to post more once I finished the book, but never did.

•

I still have my notes from the class. The night we talked about Capote, we discussed how he erases himself from the narrative, using a roving third-person point of view; the effect, Charlie said, was filmic, a series of jump-cuts. We talked about the book's sensationalism of small-town America, its nostalgic view of the Plains, how Capote seems to have an outside audience in mind. Finally, I got up the nerve to raise my hand, and asked a question about the book's shallow portrayal of the Clutters. That led into a conversation about biography, representing people, how fabrications are more readily accepted when documenting the dead. A fellow student, another fiction writer, asked a question that would echo in my head long after she said it: was Capote creating the Clutters as an all-American family, or is that who they actually were? Charlie said he was obsessed with the way texts can reveal an author's conception of where society is headed, even if they didn't mean to. Like a lot of things he said in class, that wouldn't clarify into a truth I also believed for quite some time, but I wrote myself a note: What about *In Cold Blood*? What message does it send about where society was headed?

A few days later, our term paper proposals were due. We had to post them to our course blogs for our peers to see and comment on. I knew I wanted to write about how *In Cold Blood* portrays the dead, but didn't know what angle to take, or how to begin to write a twenty-page seminar paper. So I scanned through my class notes, searching for ideas. I'm scanning through them again as I write this, pages torn out of a notebook, scrawled in capital letters, arrows and circles and stars in the margins, a record of my thoughts, Charlie's lectures, remnants of things other people said, a filtered and incomplete[9] document of the class itself. Most of it doesn't make sense now, so far from its original context: *life as trying not to die*; *the only way to describe smell is metaphor*; an inscrutable note from the week we discussed the Zapruder film about Freud and penises. But some of it still does. I can see the seeds of my fixation. The first day of the class, after watching the Holocaust documentary: *look for tendencies in trauma narratives*. Later, from our discussion of a Werner Herzog documentary: *all authors realize intentions they didn't intend to realize*. A note from the week we talked about Pennebaker, the Maysles brothers, and cinéma vérité, that says something like *the truer a document is, the less it can present a cohesive narrative*. Documentary as ethnography, a filmmaker's relationship to the Other. The concept of triage: what gets documented, what doesn't.

Eventually, I settled on a topic. *I want to write about representation of the dead in trauma narratives*, I wrote, and picked three texts to focus on: *Underground,* Haruki Murakami's book about the Tokyo subway attacks; an

---

9. Some weeks are missing, probably because I didn't go to class.

untitled short film by Ira Sachs about 9/11; and *In Cold Blood*. All three document mass murders and the collective trauma that affected large groups of people, including many who were not involved in the actual events, but they take different approaches. Murakami interviews victims. Sachs shows missing posters of the dead. *Capote*, I wrote, *just makes lots of stuff up.*

But they all have the same effect: they marginalize the dead within the documents of their own deaths. I wondered why that happened so often in stories about murder. Obviously, part of it was practical: the dead are not available to interview or observe, the main methods of documentary portrayal. You can talk to people who knew them, and build a character from those perspectives, but nobody wants to speak ill of the dead. The sign/referent relationship gets mediated in a different way; the historical person, complex and flawed and unknowable, becomes an idyll on the page. Dead people are flat characters.

•

One of my classmates in the Documentary Impulse was a guy named Morgan. He was a few years older than me, handsome, smart, well-liked, and more conversant than I with literary analysis. I would have found a reason to hate him had he not also been kind and remarkably unpretentious, considering that he was a recent MFA grad in poetry and was now pursuing another master's in literature. We weren't friends, and I didn't know him well—it seems important to say that. We had a few conversations, before class or during breaks, about the course texts, NFL football, our shared origins in the mid-Atlantic.[10] Early in the semester, he helped organize a poetry reading to raise money for survivors of Hurricane Katrina. I went, and bought a benefit chapbook that included a poem of his. I've since lost it.

Morgan's course blog is still online. He posted an audio clip of a lecture about documentary poetics,[11] the first time I heard the term. He posted an article about JetBlue's in-flight service, newly launched at the time of 9/11, which allowed passengers in the air over New York that morning to see the planes hit the towers on TV, then watch out their windows as they burned. He also posted, not long after I did, about Elliott Smith. At one point we exchanged comments about the anthropomorphism of bears in *Grizzly Man*.

Morgan had cystic fibrosis. He talked about it openly in class; one night, some of us went to a bar afterward, and he declined because of the smoke. Writing about his illness

---

10. I was born in Philadelphia, as was most of my family, although I didn't live there long. Morgan was from New Jersey.
11. The lecture is by Alan Gilbert, given at the Jack Kerouac School of Disembodied Poetics in July 2000, and is still available at the link Morgan posted: https://archive.org/details/Alan_Gilbert_lecture_on_documentary_poet_00P075.

here would be an invasion of privacy if Morgan were still alive, but he died years ago, at the age of thirty-three, and the dead don't have a right to privacy—not legally, anyway.[12] I'm making him a character based on a few brief interactions several years ago and artifacts of his life that remain online: photos, a few poems,[13] blog posts he wrote for our class. I liked Morgan, and hope it's a positive portrayal, but I can't give him the depth he deserves here. What gives me the right to portray Morgan here at all?

•

A few weeks before the class ended, *Capote* finally came to Tucson. I went to see it, and wrote a post about how the movie focused almost exclusively on the writing of *In Cold Blood*. From one angle, that made sense: the book was the "most significant endeavor of his life," as I awkwardly put it, and the reason for his lasting fame. The drama of that period of time, the difficulty of the research and writing process, allows the movie to show its subject in different lights:

---

12. This is according to my understanding, from a consultation with a lawyer about disclosing medical facts in a different nonfiction project. But I am not a lawyer, this is not advice, and so on.
13. Morgan published two books of poems, as well as multiple chapbooks, under his full name, Morgan Lucas Schuldt. You can read more about him at the website of the foundation started in his name: https://thebreathefoundation.org/about-morgan-lucas-schuldt.

Capote comes off as complex and profoundly flawed, as a good character should. And the *In Cold Blood* years present a much more manageable narrative timeline than his entire life does. The book marked the precipitous peak of his career, and cutting away from the still-famous, still-successful Truman Capote makes a satisfying ending for the movie.

But how accurate is it? The movie leaves out his turbulent, hardscrabble boyhood, alienated from his parents, living with relatives in rural Alabama; his mother's alcoholism, their tortured relationship, and her early death; his stint as an enfant terrible of the New York literary scene. Nor does it show his own descent into alcoholism and subsequent death: they're mentioned only at the end, two sentences of white letters on a black screen. When we first see Capote, he is thirty-five, sitting in a chair, snipping an article from the *New York Times*. The last time we see him, as he watches Perry Smith die, he is forty-one. Six of the sixty years he was alive.

How natural is it, I wrote, *to base a purported biography on a fraction of a life?* It struck me as a fiction writer's sensibility, like one of the cliches we threw around in workshops of short stories: how one slice of a life could define it, and stand in for the rest. It also struck me as false, because it's the kind of thing that works best (and perhaps only) when representing the dead. *Living, breathing, changing people tend not to define themselves by a single moment in their lives. Think of your own life, and see how well it works. The movie can distill*

Truman Capote to little more than a microcosm, because Truman Capote cannot contradict its representation of him, because the real Truman Capote is dead, and mostly forgotten.

My post ends with an odd digression about memoirs, which were having a cultural moment at the time. Anthony Bourdain, Dave Eggers, Alexandra Fuller, Augusten Burroughs, Azar Nafisi, Jeanette Walls, and a handful of others had recently published blockbuster memoirs; Didion's *The Year of Magical Thinking* came out halfway through our class. James Frey's *A Million Little Pieces* had just been picked for Oprah's book club, and topped bestseller lists for that entire semester. (It wouldn't last: a few weeks after the class ended, a controversy would erupt over the accuracy of Frey's book, one that colors the conversation about memoirs to this day.) I wrote that *Capote*'s approach of focusing on a particular period or aspect of the author's life seemed like a memoiristic sensibility, but without the element of authorial choice. The post ends with what I probably thought was a throwaway line, bow-tying, a stab at a practical takeaway: *You might as well write the story of your own life, so you get to distort it to suit your own aesthetic or practical considerations, and decide for yourself how you will be represented.* Note the second person: you could write nonfiction, but I was still convinced of the value of the fiction-writing enterprise, still telling all those stories about ghosts.

•

On November 15, the anniversary of the Clutter murders, our class discussed the Zapruder film. I don't have any notes from that class, and don't remember it. I might have written that night instead. That's how I used to write, binges into the witching hours. I rarely do that anymore, but I'm writing this late on the night of November 15, 2019. Sixty years ago, the Clutters were getting ready for bed. Sometime after midnight, Herb Clutter would be awakened by two strange men demanding money. Within an hour, the whole family would be dead. All these years later, what remains of them? A house in Holcomb another family lives in. Graves in Garden City. Herb and Bonnie Clutter's eldest daughters, who had moved away at the time of the murders, are still alive.[14] But most of the world remembers the Clutters from *In Cold Blood*. Page upon page of internet search results, a handful of photographs, a measure of infamy. Their names rarely appear without Capote's. The dead are frozen in time, trapped in a portrayal written by a man who never met them.

Charlie's class wrapped up with another book about the dead, about trauma, about time and memory: W.G. Sebald's *The Emigrants*. It would join a few of the other readings from that class in becoming touchstones for my writing

---

14. As of 2017, according to news coverage.

and teaching. *The Emigrants* is a nonfiction novel, in a sense: its characters seem to be representations of actual people, emigrants who fled the Holocaust by various methods and are given fictional names in the text. It includes photos, but no captions or clear explanations of them; the images of people are decontextualized portrayals, drifting on the page, signs separated from their referents, a code without a key. The narrator disappears for long stretches of the book, or seems to, and it's never clear exactly who is telling us this story; one of many questions I wrote in in my copy of *The Emigrants* was "Is the narrator Sebald?"

I didn't understand it at the time, but it was a savvy way to design a class, another thing I'd later steal from Charlie. *The Emigrants* brought the course full circle, from *Night and Fog* to another representation of the Holocaust, two very different approaches to the same grisly material. One literal, one abstract. One that claimed to be true, one that didn't. I remember someone saying something about how they served as aesthetic brackets for the other course texts, a continuum on which to locate different approaches to the Documentary Impulse. I wasn't exactly sure what that meant, but I did wonder: Where did Capote fit?

•

The end of the semester snuck up on me, like it always does.

Charlie's class closed with a discussion about the relationship between documentary film and creative nonfiction. It seems like that conversation had a profound influence on me as a writer and teacher, but I don't remember it at all, and didn't take any notes. Maybe I was absent. According to a journal I kept at the time, I went to campus health that day about worsening chest pains. The doctor listened to my heart, prodded me a little, asked if I was drinking a lot or feeling depressed. I said no more than usual. He sighed and asked if I was sleeping. I said not really. I left with a prescription for sleeping pills and a vague promise of Xanax if they didn't help.

Our seminar paper was due two weeks later. I spent most of that time grading finals for my composition classes, revising stories for my fiction workshops, and popping pills I washed down with alcohol, after which I sometimes slept for thirteen hours straight. I don't know how much to blame the Documentary Impulse for my mental state at the time. There were other factors: I lived alone in a converted garage at the end of a dark alley, obsessed about death, listened to a lot of Elliott Smith, drank too much, spent too much time alone, slept odd hours or not at all; at one point, I tried to go nocturnal, but it didn't stick. I was in the midst of an endless breakup with a classmate I'd been dating. Teaching gave me crippling anxiety. The only mail I got—and most of the interpersonal communication, given my schedule—was rejections from literary magazines. And the holidays were approaching, a time of year I hadn't liked much since my mother's death. Things were generally not going well, so it wasn't all the class's fault. But immersing myself in documentaries about dead people didn't help.

My paper was about how the dead are represented in stories that claim to be true. I'd written a short abstract and published it on my course blog. The syllabus says I was supposed to turn in a longer sketch and a draft, but I didn't. Instead I did what I'd always done for college papers: procrastinated until right before it was due, then went on a writing bender.

The first step was to actually read all of that theory I was supposed to have read months ago. I still have the handouts from that class, copies so thick they stress the staples, essays and chapters of academic books about documentary film, marked up with stars and arrows and slanted capitals; by then, I was even starting to take notes like Charlie. One of them, Michael Renov's essay "Toward a Poetics of Documentary," identifies four basic tendencies of documentary: to preserve, persuade, analyze, or express.[15] He argues that each tendency reflects a different desire on the part of the filmmaker.

The preservational mode, for instance, tries to recreate

15. The version I read is from an anthology Renov edited, *Theorizing Documentary*. New York: Routledge, 1993, 21–36. His full categories are as follows: "to record, reveal, or preserve; to persuade or promote; to analyze or interrogate; to express."
16. Renov, 25.

a more or less objective reality; it does so out of a desire "to cheat death, stop time, restore loss."[16] But reality can't be recreated: the image on film is just a sign, a representation of the object, not the object itself. Or, as Renov puts it:

> Always issues of selection intrude (which angle, take, camera stock will best serve); the results are indeed *mediated*, the result of multiple interventions that necessarily *come between* the cinematic sign (what we see on the screen) and its referent (what existed in the world).[17]

The way a filmmaker (or a writer) mediates that relationship affects the meaning of the text. Renov says preservational documentaries often try to seem objective, but that objectivity is a lie. He cites Roland Barthes, who calls objectivity "a particular form of fiction, the result of what might be called the referential illusion, where the historian tries to give the impression that the referent is speaking for itself."[18]

When I read through *In Cold Blood* again with Renov's modes in mind, I saw how it tries hard to seem objective, at least at first. It opens with a distant view of Holcomb,

---

17. Ibid, 26. The italics are his.
18. Renov quotes this from Barthes' "Historical Discourse," *Introduction to Structuralism*, ed. Michael Lane, New York: Basic Books, 1970, 149, 154.

the camera high and panning, the sort of sequence that has opened so many crime documentaries since. We see wheat fields, grain elevators, the town itself. The description is dry, detached, focusing on Holcomb's climate, location—"almost the exact middle" of America—its blue skies, clear air, main roads and major buildings.

The first character we meet is Mr. Clutter. He shows up on page five, and is described the same way as the town, in seemingly objective detail. We get his hair color (dark), his rimless eyeglasses, his exact height and weight (five-ten, one fifty-four), and age (forty-eight): the kind of facts you learn in an autopsy report, which is where Capote got them. Soon the book's portrayal of Mr. Clutter expands into an obitual biography, including his educational background (a Kansas State alumnus), financial status (not as rich as the richest man in Holcomb), and his reputation in the community (its most widely known resident). We get his ancestry, his wife and kids, a description of his house. Capote works his way into the book's first scene, a day in the life of Mr. Clutter, another establishing shot. He wakes early, drinks milk, and eats an apple as he walks across his property, which allows a cinematic view of River Valley Farm: the barns, the animals, the elms lining the driveway, and finally the river, where Mr. Clutter encounters a group of men with shotguns. They turn out to be harmless pheasant hunters, whom he wishes good hunting before touching his hatbrim and turning back. In

Renov's terms, *In Cold Blood* uses the preservational mode for Mr. Clutter, trying to bring him back to life on the page. Because his subject is dead, Capote can't interview or observe him, so he portrays Mr. Clutter—and the book almost always calls him by his surname—in journalistic terms: source-based, statistical, and supposedly objective, but also distant and clinical and superficial, like he's an exhibit in a museum. At first that seems appropriate to a book that claims to be true: just the facts, and so on. Until you turn the page and meet the killer.

When we first see Perry Smith, ten pages into the book, he's sitting in a roadside cafe. The scene has no sense of a camera slowly zooming in, no establishing shot from the sky. We're inside Smith's head by the second line: *He preferred root beer.* We learn what brand of cigarettes he smokes (Pall Mall), what he's worried about (his friend is late to meet him), that he collects maps. Smith thinks it's kind of funny, being back in Kansas, when four months earlier he'd sworn he'd never come back here. *Well, it wasn't for long.*[19] The distance of Mr. Clutter's portrayal is gone, replaced by what writing professors call free indirect discourse, when the text gives us the character's thoughts directly. It's a technique used to create intimacy, a sense of identification with a character; Capote uses it throughout *In Cold Blood*, almost exclusively

---

19. Italics are mine, 14.

with the character of Perry Smith. It's Renov's persuasive mode: the book wants you to feel sympathy for the killer. So much for objectivity.

As the book unfolds, the contrast between Capote's portrayals of Smith and the Clutter family sharpens, suggesting his agenda. The book devotes short sections to each of the victims, distant representative scenes like Mr. Clutter's: Nancy helps a protégé bake a pie, Bonnie has an awkward interaction with a houseguest, Kenyon varnishes a chest he built as a wedding guest from his sister. Within those moments, we get objective details meant to define them: their physical descriptions, their relationships to others, the objects in their bedrooms. Capote plays the Clutters to type: Herb the teetotaling Methodist who "cut a man's-man-figure" and was "always certain of what he wanted in the world"; Mrs. Clutter, the housewife who collects miniature figurines and feels an ineffable sadness; Nancy, the straight-A student, the class president who wore her boyfriend's signet ring; Kenyon, the gangly, rambunctious teenager, building contraptions, scared of girls. The full title of the book is *In Cold Blood: A True Account of a Multiple Murder and Its Consequences*, but it devotes just thirty-five of 343 pages to the victims. In the story of their own murders, the victims get reduced, shrunk in scale, like the gewgaws Bonnie Clutter keeps in her dining room, so small they could fit in a shoebox. So much for consequences.

•

Another theory text Charlie had us read was a chapter of Bill Nichols' book *Representing Reality* about portrayals of real people, or, as Nichols puts it: "The recurring question of what to do with people, of how to *represent* another person when any representation threatens diminution, fabrication, and distortion."[20] That question is especially difficult to answer when representing *dead* people, and more so for victims of violence. Nichols mentions a documentary[21] that opens with the bodies of four murdered women, and asks a series of questions that would preoccupy me for years to come:

> What ethical (or political) perspective authorizes such a sight? What response can we as viewers have? What effort is called for to restore the full magnitude of a life that has reached its termination? By what means and to what ends can the absent life be given representation, however incomplete and partial?[22]

In my paper, I argued that Capote mediated the sign/referent relationship in a way that distanced the viewer from the victims, diminishing the magnitude of their lives. A book

---

20. Italics are his, 231.
21. *Roses in December.* I haven't seen it.
22. This quote has been slightly condensed. Nichols, 233.

that claimed to be the true story of a murder focused not on the real people who were killed, but the trauma their deaths caused the living. The dead were pushed to the margins, the victims silenced. The importance of authorial intent had been passé for decades by then—Roland Barthes announced the death of the author the year after *In Cold Blood* came out[23]—so my paper didn't address an obvious question: *Why* did Capote write the Clutters that way? It acknowledged only one possible reason, a practical concern: the Clutters were not available for interviews or observation, because they were dead and buried by the time Capote arrived in Kansas. Every description *In Cold Blood* gives of them is based on someone else's testimony. The funeral home scene, for example, comes from Capote's interview of Susan Kidwell, but the description of the Clutters' bodies is pure Capote: "The head of each was completely encased in cotton, a swollen cocoon twice the size of an ordinary blown-up balloon, and the cotton, because it had been sprayed with a glossy substance, twinkled like Christmas-tree snow."[24] Even in death, the Clutters are faceless, sanitized, symbolic.

My paper petered out toward the end, and never quite said what the reader should take away from it. Searching for an exit, I quoted Nichols again, about the Othering of the

---

23. Capote probably disagreed; he had little use for critics or critical theory, and in interviews about his work (as well as the work itself) he often seems to think that his intent was the only thing that mattered.
24. Capote, 95.
25. Nichols, 234. Italics mine.

dead: *Victims and martyrs float in the timeless realm of the ill-fated or exemplary.*[25] The closest thing to an argument is the last paragraph, which presented what I somewhat grandiosely called an ethical imperative:

> In documenting the dead, or the events that caused their deaths, they must receive the same fundamental human respect as the living. If we allow the dead to be exhumed anytime a documentarian wishes to employ them in the symbology of larger social issues, we trivialize the significance of their deaths, and by extension the value of their lives. If the dead are marginalized within the documents of their own traumas, then their lives themselves lose their meaning.

Technically, that's not the last paragraph. I might have been riding a writing high when I finished, or I might have been drinking coffee in the middle of the night in my alleyway apartment, something the vanished version of me who wrote the paper often did. I don't know why, but I wrote an afterword, four more pages under the heading "Alternatives and Implications: Toward an Ethics of Representation." It reads like the work of someone who's just pulled an all-nighter writing his first graduate paper. There's some stuff about the cultural marketplace and capital-intensive modes of production, the role of the documentarian in a disposable culture. It asks what I must have thought was a profound question: *What does it mean to be dead?* Near the end, I meditated on death and genre: *representing the dead is an extraliminal space on the genre map, beyond the capacities of documentary, beyond the authority of fiction.* Finally, I brought it all back to my own writing: I mentioned a fiction project about a traumatic event similar to Capote's subject matter. I must have known I wanted to write about my mother's murder, but I couldn't bring myself to say it yet. That would take a few more years.

•

I got an A in the class, and figured that was that. I forgot about Capote and went back to writing short stories. A few weeks later, I decided to write one about an old stepdad of mine; he wasn't the one who killed my mother, but he had been violent, and I remembered him as a villain, at least until I started to write about him.

The story, "Tortolita," is about a guy name Andy. He's in his mid-twenties, his mother is dead, and he lives in Tucson in a studio apartment; he's pretty much me at the time. One day a real estate circular comes in the mail, and on it he sees a photo of his former stepdad, Alex, who is pretty much my former stepdad; I didn't even change his name. Andy goes to see him, and a series of conflicts ensue, climaxing in a pellet-gun showdown in the cul de sac of a tract-home subdivision way out in the desert.

The story felt different from my others. The characters *seemed* real, because they were, and so did the place, because it was, too. For the first time in my life, the voice on the page felt like mine. It was also the first thing I'd ever written that I thought might be good. I took it as a sign, and started writing truer stories.

I finished my master's, and the university let me stay on as an adjunct lecturer, the academic equivalent of working in the service industry, which I also did: at nights, after teaching, I tended bar. Sometimes I'd see Charlie around Modern Languages, and we'd stop to chat in the hallway. He came into the bar once or twice, and I'd comp him a beer if the boss wasn't around. We weren't friends yet, but now the possibility existed.

I'd come home from bar shifts at three in the morning and write until the sky over the campus went white. I sent stories to lit mags, got rejections back, pinned them to the wall above my writing desk, stared up and dreamed of something coming through, like the cliché of a failed writer I was fast becoming. I started a novel, out of some dim sense that it was what a real writer would do, but I couldn't figure out what happened next, on the page or in real life. Grad school was over. I'd made it through six years of college thanks to my mother's life insurance payout, and that money was gone. So were most of my friends, who'd gone back to the places they came from, and I was thinking about doing the same, applying for jobs teaching high school or being a cop, constructing dubious late-night internet dreams about joining the Peace Corps or teaching English abroad. I was desperate for material, some big experience to write about that wasn't the only one I'd ever had: my mother's murder. One afternoon, while I was in the shower, getting ready for a shift at the bar, my phone rang. I toweled off, checked my messages, and heard a grave Irish voice informing me that I'd been chosen for a Stegner Fellowship.

Known as the Stegner among my MFA classmates, the fellowship was a common barstool dream, two years of getting paid to write. I didn't understand what a fellowship was, exactly, and pride wouldn't allow me to ask, but I'd gathered that you got to go to Stanford and study with famous writers. One of our professors had been a Stegner, and so had a classmate's spouse, and sometimes they would talk in hushed tones about how great of a time it was. To me the Stegner was a distant star, one of the ones that might be Pluto. Everyone applied, and a few months later we'd commiserate over our rejections over beers at the Red Garter. But nobody *got* one.

I called a couple of my writer friends to see if they were fucking with me. Then I called back, and spoke to the program assistant, who assured me that it wasn't a mistake. I ran around my apartment, naked and screaming, until I realized I still had to go to work. I came home in the middle of the night to messages of congratulation. The next day, I was daydreaming down a hallway in Modern Languages when Charlie shouted from the far end to stop me, and met me in the middle to shake my hand. He seemed almost as happy about the fellowship as I was. He had lived in the Bay Area for years, while doing his doctorate at Berkeley, and offered to give me pointers. I needed pointers, having never lived in a city so big and rich and foreign; he must have understood that, even if I didn't. We met for lunch at a cheesesteak place, and I don't remember what we talked about, but we met, and talked, and treated each other like normal people for the first time, outside the context of a classroom. He even went to the impromptu going-away outing a few friends arranged for me, which turned into the sort of shameful, debauched all-nighter Capote would have appreciated.

Maybe that was the beginning, the first step to becoming friends. Maybe Charlie's class was the beginning of my obsession with *In Cold Blood*, and how murder stories treat victims. Those events came first, and suggest a clean, chronological story, which is how we like to believe things happened in the past. And it's true, more or less: these things happened, these people existed. Still, somehow telling it feels like a lie. In life, this was a random sequence of events, just some shit that happened with no clear sense of cause and effect. Turning it into a story makes it seem inevitable, preordained: I met Charlie in undergrad, took his class in grad school, read *In Cold Blood*, wrote a paper about how it marginalizes the dead, and then a story that did the same thing, which I sent as an application sample to Stanford. They let me in, and I went, and eventually that led me here, to writing this book about Truman Capote. It's clear, neat, sensical. A good story.

But is it true? All of this could have easily happened another way, and seemed just as inevitable in retrospect. In a more probable past, I kept bartending, became a high school teacher or a cop, stopped writing. Or I didn't get into grad school at all, dropped out of college, never went. In a much more likely past, I wound up in jail, like a lot of my childhood friends, or hooked on opioids, or dead, or all of the above, like my uncle, the one everybody always said I was like.

Instead I wound up what I am now, more than a decade removed from the Documentary Impulse: a writing professor at a big state university, a knockoff Charlie teaching students like the one I used to be. I draw the same kind of diagrams he did on the board, say the same sort of gnomic things about literature. Mostly I teach nonfiction, how to tell a true story. How to make yourself a narrator, a prism the reader thinks is a mirror. I spend a lot of time trying to explain that the person on the page is not the author, not a person at all. It's a performance, a storyteller, a selector of information—what to tell and what not to, what to save for later to create suspense. A signmaker, the key to the code. Sometimes, like here, the act is explicit, an I on the page; sometimes the narrator hides behind the third person, like Capote's. Either way, it's an act. I have to remind my students all the time: *This is a narrator. This is a narrator. This is a narrator.*

And what about my big question? How do you write the dead? Not many students ask me that. If they do, I might point them to a moment in Sebald's *The Emigrants*, the last reading from Charlie's class, when our mysterious narrator flips through a book of photos left behind by a man who killed himself:

> *Again and again, from front to back and from back to front, I leafed through the album that afternoon, and since then I have returned to it time and again, because, looking at the picture in it, it truly seemed to me, and still does, as if the dead were coming back, or we were on the point of joining them.*[26]

---

26. This is the New Directions paperback of the English translation, published in 1996. Sebald, 45–46.

PART II

Creation Myths

THE STORY OF *IN COLD BLOOD* goes something like this: in November of 1959, Truman Capote was flipping through the *New York Times* when he saw an article about the brutal murders of a family in rural Kansas. At thirty-five, Capote was already the renowned author of a handful of books, both fiction and nonfiction, as well as plays, screenplays, short stories, and journalism. The year before, his novella, *Breakfast at Tiffany's*, had been a success, and it would soon become an iconic film. His career was going remarkably well, but he was artistically restless. He wanted to do something entirely new, journalism written like fiction, what he called the "nonfiction novel." He'd been waiting for the right subject; the unsolved killing of the Clutter family fit the bill. He pitched the idea to his editor at the *New Yorker*, got the green light, went to Kansas, and followed the case for the next five years, through the arrest of the killers, their trial and appeals, finally their hangings. *In Cold Blood*'s four sections were serialized in *The New Yorker* in late 1965 to sensational acclaim. The book was published by Random House soon after, began a long stay at the top of bestseller lists, and quickly became an American classic.

Capote would tell that story over and over again after the book's release, but, like the book itself, it's dubiously true. He continued to revise and embellish the origin myth of *In Cold Blood* over the six years he spent writing it, and during its long afterlife, as the book begot a complicated legacy. Part of that was financial: global book and movie rights for *In Cold Blood* made Capote two million dollars before it was even published, or, as the *New York Times* put it, "fourteen dollars and eight cents a word."[27] The book has been called the second-best-selling true crime book of all time, which seems like a matter of interpretation.[28] *In Cold Blood* certainly made Capote enough money to set himself up in style: he soon bought a new Jaguar and an apartment in Manhattan with a river view, his main residence for the rest of his life.

When Capote died in 1984, after a slow and ignominious decline, he left his estate to his longtime partner, Jack Dunphy, with instructions to turn it into a trust after Jack's

---

27. *Capote*, 363.
28. In terms of what bestselling means, absolute or relative numbers, as well as what true crime means, which is a whole other can of worms.

death. The Truman Capote Literary Trust was established in 1994, and immediately gave large donations to creative writing programs at prominent universities, including one to Stanford, which used it to establish more creative writing fellowships like the one I received. In other words, *In Cold Blood* helped pay for my writerly education.[29]

And what an education it was. Have you ever *been* to Stanford? I printed out directions before I drove from Arizona, and only once I arrived did I see what a rube I'd been to think that you could miss it. I turned off the 280 at the sign and followed a phalanx of luxury cars to a campus unlike any campus I had ever seen: sandstone arches, mile-long lawns, bell towers and tour buses, sculptures and cathedrals and shit, like the fiefdom of some storybook lord. I parked my nine-year-old Volkswagen on the quad and took a picture; of what, exactly, I didn't know. Of Stanford. It was my first time in Northern California, and I was such a tourist.

But Capote was right: writing a true story is a matter of selection, and one thing I learned pretty quickly about having a coveted fellowship was not to talk about it much. The relevant part here is that, two years after Charlie's class and a thousand miles away, the documentary impulse reared its head again.

---

29. This is only indirectly true: the fellowships are named after their benefactors, and I was not a Truman Capote Fellow. But if the Capote Trust's donation hadn't allowed the program to expand, I might not have gotten in.

I was a few months into the fellowship, and reprising my graduate school experience in perhaps too many ways: sleeping odd hours, drinking too much, cultivating crushes on classmates, struggling to fit in with my more worldly peers. In others, I was making the most of it. I sponged as much as I could from the brilliant people around me, the way they talked about writing, the culture they knew, obscure books and music and movies. I went to writer parties, dinners at the estates of donors, readings by famous authors. I even weaseled my way into a weekly writer basketball game at a secret court overlooking the Castro, at which, one week, I guarded Dave Eggers, whose memoir had meant more to me as a young and recently orphaned man than I could convey during a postgame handshake. I spent my first few months in California basking in the freedom and good fortune that had been afforded me, trying to appreciate my brief time among the chosen. The only problem was the reason I was there in the first place: I couldn't write anything worth a damn.

I was still writing fiction, or trying to. I'd sent the only two good stories I had as the sample for the fellowship, but they were autobiographical, the sort of juvenilia I thought I should leave behind now that I'd moved up to journeyman. The first thing I wrote in California was a story about a priest in World War II, which it took me months to realize was probably a novel, and not one I was capable of writing. At first I thought maybe it was just the same old self-doubt, my white-trash inferiority complex at work. So I turned some of it in for workshop, to see what other people said, and everyone was nice about it, but the answer was obvious. In retrospect, it makes sense: I was young, hadn't been writing that long, hadn't read enough. Some of my new friends tactfully tried to explain that to me, but it didn't get through. It felt like I was failing, fucking up, blowing my lottery-ticket chance at some golden life where I got to live in San Francisco and go to Stanford. The fellowship didn't have strings attached, but the idea was that you were there to write, to produce *something*, and I thought constantly about all those other writers who had applied for my spot. It was the first time I'd ever felt pressure to write, to succeed, to belong among the best young writers in the country. I wasted the first year on fiction nobody would ever read. But I was learning how to be a writer, all the same.

I'd like to be able to say I had an epiphany, like Capote, and came up with the idea of trying something different on my own. But a teacher had to tell me. It was Colm Toíbín, an Irish writer who visited Stanford for one quarter while I was there. Colm cut a Capote-ish figure: short, handsome, gay, and brilliant, with a divisive personality and a distinctive voice, although his was a washboard brogue, not Capote's oft-imitated lisp. And, like Capote, Colm knew how to throw a party. Visiting writers were given lodging on Stanford's campus, the former estate of a railroad tycoon known with smug demureness as the Farm, but the bucolic life was not for Colm, who instead rented an apartment near the Castro, with a deck overlooking the city, where we'd all go get drunk with him and his famous writer friends. He didn't have to invite us—I probably wouldn't have—but he did, because that's the kind of guy he is.

He was also funny and blunt, often both at the same time, a dangerous combination in a writing workshop. Colm came from a different tradition of literary mentorship than we were used to. He didn't have an MFA, and seemed to have a thinly veiled contempt for the way writing was taught in America. Colm pulled no punches: he'd read our work in class, aloud, and in the parts he thought were bad, his voice went high and sharp, a needle puncturing your hopes and pretensions.

I don't know why I liked him so much, but I did. Maybe it was that Colm was fucking *funny*, and probably the least pretentious writer I had ever met. Maybe it was his work. His latest book, a short story collection, had just come out.[30] A story from it, "One Minus One," had been in *The New Yorker*, and we'd all read it before he arrived. "One Minus One" is about a man walking through a city under a full Texas moon, on the sixth anniversary of his mother's death, and remembering her. That's the story, more or less. But the

---

30. The US paperback edition, which included "One Minus One"—I don't think the hardcover did.

clarity, the precision, the feeling in the rhythms of the lines; reading it was like following a flashlight beam down the dark trail of grief. I read it not long after the sixth anniversary of my mother's death, a night on which I went to see the writer Steve Almond give a reading in the Haight, then walked home through a still-strange city, feeling the same thing the narrator of Colm's story does—*the bitter past has come back to me in these alien streets in a way that feels like violence.*[31] Years later, Almond would write one of the books in this series; that night, he told a story about meeting Kurt Vonnegut, who another book in this series is about. That's how that time in my life feels to me now, a decade later, like an era of invisible coincidences. At some point around then, Alan U. Schwartz, the executor of the Truman Capote Trust, gave a talk at Stanford about privacy and copyright; I think I shook his hand afterward, maybe even had a brief conversation. My memory of that night isn't clear. Maybe it didn't seem important. A lot of things didn't at the time.

"One Minus One" was the kind of story I wished I could write about my mother's death. It captured being six years removed from losing her, right down to the sense that I'd stepped out of reality since, that her death was, as Colm put it, "the last real thing that happened to me."[32] I liked the story so much I asked him about it in workshop. "Fuck it,"

---

31. *Mothers and Sons*, first paperback edition, Scribner, 2008, 274. This line is edited from the original.
32. Ibid.

he said. "I just told the truth." He said he was walking down a street one night in Austin, Texas, and a voice came to him, the intimate second person of that story, me speaking to you. Once you have the voice, he said, you wait until you have a plot, and then you write it all down.

Inspired, I handed in my own story about my mother's death for workshop. In class, Colm leafed through the manuscript, page by page, and tore it apart, crossing out paragraphs and reading lines of bad dialogue in a sardonic tone it still stings to remember, over a decade later. I was sitting right next to him. My classmates cringed and kindly tried to interrupt or redirect him, but it didn't work, and I didn't want them to. It was exactly what I needed, someone to tell me what I was doing wrong, someone who cared enough to do it, even if it meant I might hate him for it. I didn't hate him for it. I didn't know much about writing or teaching, but I knew a gift when I saw it. At the end of the workshop, Colm leaned into the table, pulled his glasses low on his nose, and gave one of his nuggets of advice: "What occupies you emerges in your work," he said. "You have to go there. You have to put it down. Otherwise you'll just keep circling and circling." This guy's mom is dead, he said, tapping the page. Write about *that*.

That's how Colm was as a teacher: blunt, irreverent, apothegmatic. He told us you had to look at a story at different times of day: *what you've written in the dark looks different in the light.* He said it was easier to write about the dead: their deadness meant the story was yours to tell. He said writers shouldn't keep secrets: you have to write about them, no matter who it offends, because secrets make the best stories. Colm didn't just resemble Capote: he shared his aesthetic.

•

Truman Capote was a literary wunderkind. He was supposedly convinced of his future career path by the age of eleven, and he started pursuing it while he was still in high school, when he got a copy job at *The New Yorker.* The thirties and forties were a golden era for American short fiction, when magazines paid authors significant money to publish stories, and some made a living doing it.

Capote launched his career based on a few early stories he published in national magazines like *Harper's Bazaar* and *Mademoiselle*, which were prominent outlets for literary fiction at the time. At the age of twenty, he walked into the offices of *Mademoiselle*, manuscript in hand, and demanded that someone read it; that someone turned out to be Rita Smith, who soon published another of his stories, "Miriam," which won a prestigious O. Henry Award and established Capote as a rising young talent. Smith later introduced him to her sister, Carson McCullers, who was then the lioness of Southern letters. McCullers got Capote into Yaddo, the exclusive artist residency in upstate New York, and introduced him to agents and editors. One of the latter was a senior editor at Random House, who saw potential in "Miriam" and bought his first book before it was even written. Capote was twenty-one at the time.[33]

Then as now, literary success was largely a matter of an author's talent for self-promotion. Capote was the best there's ever been. Before his first novel came out, he'd already been prominently featured in a *Life* magazine spread about the best young American writers. That debut, *Other Voices, Other Rooms*, got mixed reviews—most of his books would—but it was an instant bestseller, thanks to a controversy over Capote's author photo, a suggestive shot of the boyish author reclining on a couch; his biographer said the photo "probably caused more comment than his prose."[34] His next book of fiction, *Breakfast at Tiffany's*, was an even bigger success.[35] His third, *The Grass Harp*, was a runner-up for the National Book Award.

By the time he first read about the Clutter murders, Capote was already a famous author. How famous is hard to

33. These events are paraphrased from Clarke's *Capote*.
34. Clarke, Gerald. *Capote*. Simon & Schuster, 1988. Pg. 158.
35. The movie changed the plot significantly, and Capote didn't like it. He also wanted Marilyn Monroe to play Holly Golightly, not Audrey Hepburn.

say. He wasn't anyone's idea of a major American writer, not like some of his contemporaries, Mailer or Cheever or Roth, although that had as much to do with the homophobia of the time than the quality of the other author's books. But Capote was much better than they were at cultivating fame, and was constantly the talk of the New York publishing world, which was, and still is, insular and provincial. He kept his name out there with constant bylines in magazines, and published six books by the time he turned thirty-five.[36] His contemporaries tended to agree, often grudgingly, that Capote was one of the most recognizable writers of their era, a charmer, a preternatural gossip, a master befriender, a mover and shaker. He had connections everywhere he went: on his way to Holcomb for the first time, he stopped at Kansas State to give a talk, at the invitation of the university's president, who was friends with Capote's editor at Random House.

Before *In Cold Blood*, Capote seemed to have more fame than talent. He isn't generally remembered for his early fiction, and it's easy to see why. Even as a young writer, his prose was exceptional, the product of an aspiring stylist, lean and ironic, with a masterful sense of rhythm. But the stories are shallow, sentimental, contrived, even childish, and his

---

36. In 1963, Modern Library released a collected works of Truman Capote, chosen by the author himself. He was thirty-eight at the time.

novels feel slight, more like novellas in length and depth, still skimming the surface. There's a reason he's remembered for *In Cold Blood*, and, before that, was best known for being Truman Capote.

Nor was Capote the stranger to nonfiction he would later pretend to have been. Early on, he published short travel essays; his third book, *Local Color*, was a collection of them, which sold poorly and was soon forgotten. Between his second and third novels, he published *The Muses Are Heard*, a sort of nonfiction novella, a long and gossipy account of an American ballet company's trip to Leningrad that reads like a dry run for *In Cold Blood*. Like the latter, the former was originally printed in *The New Yorker* and later released as a book by Random House, and was reckless in its portrayals of real people. Soon after, Capote wrote an infamous[37] profile of Marlon Brando, also for *The New Yorker*, that portrayed the most famous actor of his generation as a fat, balding bore, broke and paranoid, and was nearly a coffin nail for Brando's career.[38] Early in 1959, Capote published a long autobiographical essay about his time in Brooklyn, and later that year he spiked a journalistic piece about Westernized

37. And, it must be said, appallingly racist in its portrayal of Japanese people.
38. The director of the film Brando was doing at the time claimed Capote had it in for his star from the moment he arrived in Tokyo; after the article, Brando said he would kill Capote, and sank into a mid-career malaise from which he wouldn't fully recover until *The Godfather*.

youth in Russia, out of fear that it might get his subjects thrown in a gulag or killed.

Capote wasn't just moonlighting in another genre, writing nonfiction to help promote his novels, the way many literary writers approach nonfiction. By the time he heard about the Clutter murder, Capote was having an artistic crisis. In a letter from that time, he compared nonfiction— he called it "fact," which he would later understand to be a very different thing—to a box of chocolates in another room. "I realized that I was in terrible trouble as a fiction writer," he wrote. As he put it to a reporter around that time: "I like having the truth be the truth, so I don't have to change it."[39]

·

I had never really tried to write about my mother until Colm suggested it, for a lot of reasons. Six years after the fact, her murder still seemed too big to approach: I didn't think I could do it justice. I thought I'd moved on from it, still thought that was possible, and the last thing I wanted to do was re-live that time in my life. I'd absorbed a lot of American nonsense about masculine grief, so it's not surprising that I refused to acknowledge mine. And I'd learned by then what being associated with a murder victim brings you, a grim

---

39. Clarke, 317.

and piteous celebrity, a stain you can never wash out. Years earlier, I'd stumbled across an article by Eric Schlosser[40] that describes it better than I can:

> The fear of murder has grown so enormous in the United States that it leaves a taint, like the mark of Cain, on everyone murder touches. One might expect that the families of murder victims would be showered with sympathy and support, embraced by their communities. But in reality they are far more likely to feel isolated, fearful, and ashamed, overwhelmed by grief and guilt, angry at the criminal-justice system, and shunned by their old friends. America's fascination with murder has not yet extended to its aftermath.

I knew next to nothing about writing a book, but I knew enough about murder to know that if I wrote about my mother's, that book would follow me around forever. It had happened to Capote, and he never even met the Clutters.

If writing about murder had been purely a matter of choice, like Capote says it was for him, I might never have done it. In an alternate life, one I sometimes daydream

---

40. "A Grief Like No Other," from *The Atlantic Monthly*, September, 1997. Schlosser's article did more to clarify what murder means in American culture than anything else I've read. I once told him that, or tried to, after a reading he gave for another book. He said it was his favorite article he'd ever written, and probably the least read.

about, I went on to finish that book of short stories about Tombstone, published it somewhere, and tried to scrape together a career teaching fiction, like some of my classmates. But Colm told me I had to write the truth, and he was right: you do have to write what compels you. I'd been circling it for years in a decaying orbit. On one hand, I didn't think writing should be therapy, and didn't respect anyone who did; on the other, I had tried therapy, and it didn't work. I didn't think about my mother much, could barely remember her, and I was starting to see where all that stoicism would lead me, shipwrecked on some island of grief. There were other reasons: frustration with the apprentice quality of my fiction, desperation to write *something* good, grandiose notions about changing how we think and talk about murder. But I started writing about my mother's death because Colm told me to, and because I had to do something with my grief if I wanted to survive.

At first, I didn't think of it as a book. I was moonlighting, experimenting with nonfiction. The writing came easier than I'd expected, maybe because I didn't think about who might read it. Writing was a pleasant, private chore, like cooking myself a meal. It seemed to improve my mental state, and maybe my life in general: my mood improved, and it was easier to see how lucky I was, easier to enjoy the charmed Californian life I'd been given. I didn't tell anybody I was writing about my mother's death, or that I was writing nonfiction at all, and I liked being the only one who knew it existed.[41]

In the meantime, I kept going to workshop, gleaning talent, and hanging out with Colm, an education unto itself. One night, on his rooftop patio, I bummed a cigarette off a friend of his who'd just won the Booker Prize. Another, Colm recited Elizabeth Bishop's "The Moose" in its entirety, at one in the morning, in the corner of the nicest kitchen I had ever seen, while a dozen drunken writers watched in awe. Another night, at Stanford, one of those canape receptions that blur together in my memory—soft light, tablecloths, bartenders who didn't care when I told them I'd been a bartender a year before—I blundered into a conversation Colm was having with the visiting writer who'd just read. I had recently decided I should network more; when in Rome and what not. As soon as I introduced myself to her, Colm launched into a whole bit about how I was a pervert who liked to lure little girls into my basement.[42] Another time he started class with an unprompted soliloquy making fun of American writers for how much they love Chekhov, which ended with him repeating the title of his most famous story,

---

41. Writing this has reminded me how much I love this stage of a book, when it's still my secret.

42. This bears further explanation: my roommate and I had been looking for an occupant for our third bedroom, a sort of windowless burrow downstairs. The only person willing to pay $900 to live with us and without natural light was a French pharmaceutical intern in her early twenties. It was her first time living outside of her parents' home in Marseilles,

"The Lady and the Dog," over and over, moving his head from side to side, flapping his hands and cackling, almost dancing in his chair.[43]

Colm talked a lot of shit—it was one of the things I liked best about him—and held nothing sacred except writing. He was confident in his own talent, and in his beliefs about writing and books, in a way I desperately wanted to be. He was also warm, kind, generous, and perceptive: I think he saw that I was lost, and he tried to help, even though he didn't have to, and knew I couldn't return the favor. It may be too convenient to compare Colm to Capote, but I've been reading a lot about the latter, and hearing his friends describe him, he sounds a lot like Colm.

I don't want to overstate things: I didn't know Colm well, or for very long. Winter ended, he left, and we exchanged the occasional email for a while, then stopped; as I write this, I haven't spoken to him in years. But I knew him at a critical time, and, like Charlie before him, Colm had a large and lasting impact on the writer I became.

•

and she spoke only a few words of English when she moved in, but our roommateship was entirely chaste and unperverse; in fact, it became sort of a *Perfect Strangers* situation.

43. One more thing we agreed on: I can't stand that story.

I kept writing about my mother until the summer, when I went to Bread Loaf, a summer writing conference I had applied to after hearing other writers talk about it reverently. I didn't know much about it, only its reputation as a place all the famous writers went, along with agents and editors and literary New York. Once I got there, I saw pretty quick what it really was: the snootiest writers' conference in America, a feudal society where some buildings were off limits, where plebes like me had to literally wait on older, more important writers, all while constantly being told what an honor it was, an assurance that rang hollow to anyone who'd worked in the service industry as much as I had. I hated it so much that I couldn't hide it, and was eventually asked to leave. I didn't know it at the time, but that put me in good company: Capote also got kicked out of Bread Loaf, for walking out in the middle of a reading by Robert Frost. But before I left the Mountain, as it insists on calling itself, I met a writer who would play McCullers to my Capote.

I recognized her name from a story of hers I'd read about a writer with a dead mother; it seems clear now, although it didn't then, that I was a connoisseur of dead-mother stories. I told her I'd loved it, that my mother was dead, and she had gotten the feeling right. She said that's because it was all true. She asked what I was working on, and I told her about the thing I'd started writing in Colm's class, which I couldn't bring myself to call a book. She asked to read it and I sent her what I had, a few chapters, maybe forty pages.

In retrospect, I don't know why she helped me, another guy talking about his own writing at a conference lousy with them. I didn't ask for help—I had too much pride for that—and there was nothing in it for her. The only reason I could think of is the same reason I'd settled on for why Colm had helped me: we were part of the fraternity, larger and more powerful than you might think, of writers with dead mothers. Whatever her reasons, she introduced me to an agent, and to a senior editor at Random House, and a few months later the former would sell my book to the latter for more money than I had made in my entire life.

It seemed like a bad business decision, even to me. I was twenty-seven years old, had never written anything of consequence, and wasn't nearly as sure that I could as they seemed to be. I thought about saying no, and waiting until the book was done. But my mother didn't raise a fool: it was the ticket to the life I'd dreamed of as a kid, as a line cook at a tourist steakhouse, a bartender with an MFA. It meant I was a real writer, with a real book—and from Random House, no less, Capote's publisher. The money meant a future of not having to worry about rent or health insurance, that I might never have to wait on some rich asshole again. So I took it.

•

What does any of this have to do with Capote? Other than some minor literary coincidences, not much. The same sequence of events might have happened if I'd never read *In Cold Blood*. But that's how nonfiction works: the connections aren't as clear as they are in a novel. Real life doesn't work that way. You have to impose some kind of order, a logic for the story. If not for Capote, I might still have wound up at Stanford, might still have written a book. But I might not have, and it wouldn't have been the book I wrote.

One of the things I stole from the writers I was surrounded by back then was to keep notes on the books I read. In my battered copy of *In Cold Blood*, the same one I read in Charlie's class, on the blank pages at the back, are notes from what must have been my second read, in August of 2010, the month before my book was due to Random House. By then, some demon had taken the wheel: I was an exhausted conduit, cranking out thousands of words a day. So perhaps it's not surprising that my reading notes are not very insightful. I commented on the structure, the way Capote withholds information, especially the murder itself, to manufacture tension; I don't know if I stole that from him or not, but my book does the same thing.

That second time through, I also noticed new things. So much of *In Cold Blood* seemed staged, convenient, maybe invented. And Capote had so much sympathy for Perry Smith, spent so much time trying to analyze—or even justify—why he killed the Clutters. Writing a book about a victim must have clarified some things for me about murder stories. It wasn't just that Capote portrayed the victims shallowly: he barely portrayed them at all. What was supposed to be a story about the victims and their community instead became the story of their killer.

I also realized how much Capote's book had influenced mine. I hadn't set out to do it, but I'd written a response to *In Cold Blood*, a murder book about the victim. And like Capote's book defined the rest of his life, so too would mine. Not long after I handed it in, I applied for a job teaching nonfiction in New Mexico. My time at Stanford was ending, and the latest tech boom was ruining San Francisco, so when they called to offer me the job, I took it, and moved to Albuquerque to teach a genre I had never formally studied and didn't know much about. One of my first tasks was to come up with my first graduate-level literature class; the only requirement was that it focused on nonfiction. I was tempted to steal Charlie's class from stem to stern, but I came up with my own. The only thing I took from the Documentary Impulse was one of the course texts: for the first time, I would be teaching *In Cold Blood*.

PART III

Murder Tourism
in Middle America

JUST WEST OF HOLCOMB, KANSAS, on the lonesome wheat plains *In Cold Blood* begins with, stands the world's largest slaughterhouse.[44] It was the first thing Bonnie and I found when we went looking for the Clutter farm, on a June day so hot it felt like we were being ironed. Earlier, in Albuquerque, I'd typed Holcomb into my phone, and the directions led us here. If the Tyson plant had existed when Capote came to Kansas, his book would probably start with the abattoir at the edge of town. Subtlety was not his strong point.

I stopped the car at the gates of the facility, where signs prohibited trespassing. The building ahead was long and beige and bland, as if designed to hide its purpose, processing six thousand cattle a day, each shot once in

---

44. It was the world's largest when it was built in the 1980s; it has since been eclipsed.

the head. From a hundred yards away, with our windows raised against the heat, we could smell the death inside. The vegan riding shotgun didn't react how I would've expected, not a word about that one documentary on the beef industry. Bonnie just said we must've missed a turn somewhere, and she was right. We doubled back and soon found Holcomb proper.

The first paragraph of *In Cold Blood* establishes Capote's eye-of-god narration, panning across the high plains, remote and desolate, "a lonesome area that other Kansas call 'out there.'" Soon Holcomb appears in the distance, its grain elevators "rising as gracefully as Greek temples" from the wheat, a simile about as subtle as a neon sign: this is a tragedy. Capote describes the town from a detached, cinematic perspective typical of the book, all facts and landmarks, the illusion of objectivity. Dirt roads and deserted dance halls, an air of dilapidation, dry in both senses of the word. Occasional freight trains. A new school. How it might look to an outsider, tourists like us. As we drove through town, Capote's description still rang mostly true: "an aimless congregation of buildings" wedged between Route 50 and the Arkansas River, split by the tracks of the Santa Fe Railway.

A few things had changed in the fifty-odd years since Capote showed up. A modest park at the city limits, across the street from a new school, was dedicated to the memory of the Clutter family. Hartman's Cafe, the gathering place and gossip node Capote frequented, was now a Mexican restaurant called El Rancho, a signal of the demographic shift brought on by the meat industry. South of town, across the ditch that used to be the river, steam plumed from a palatial power plant. Otherwise, Holcomb looked like the rest of Kansas, hot and brown and level, scattered silos and grain elevators, water towers and windbreaks, an architecture of attempts to break the flatness.

At least that's how it seemed to me. Locals might not feel the same. Bonnie and I were tourists, full of ignorant assumptions, seeing everything relative to our frame of reference. We'd come from a city at the base of the Sandia range, where the skyline looks like a monitored heartbeat, so the flat ring of this strange horizon felt like time itself, a noose drawing tight. A week earlier, Bonnie had asked if I wanted to drive with her to Minnesota. Her brother had been picked up by a pro soccer team in the Twin Cities and needed someone to deliver his car. Our relationship was new, and discordantly defined, so a four-day trip together seemed like a bad idea. But it was summer in Albuquerque, all glare and ennui, a good time for bad ideas. The internet's suggested route ran close by Holcomb, so I said yes, as long as we could make a detour.

•

Holcombites took exception to Capote's book, especially its treatment of the Clutters, and Bonnie in particular. *In Cold Blood* portrays her as timorous, frail, depressive, frequently institutionalized. Many who knew her, including her surviving family, have claimed Capote exaggerated her condition. If so, it worked. Bonnie comes off as a more sympathetic character than her husband or children, more human and complex. I didn't see it until my second read: Capote made the other Clutters flat and stereotypical, but not Bonnie. She's stricken by an unspeakable sadness, full of doubt and anxiety; her character has a rich, unknowable depth. She dreamed of being a nurse, suffered crippling postnatal depressions, once spent two months in Wichita without her family, which she enjoyed so much the guilt drove her back. She refused to cook, and slept in a separate room from her husband. She was the only Clutter who drank coffee, and may have been the source of the mysterious cigarette smell in the house, another of Capote's gothic details, a mystery for which he never provides an answer.[45] Bonnie's prone to cryptic, ominous remarks: when we first see her, in the only scene where she takes center stage, she makes a series of unsettling suggestions to a houseguest, her daughter's friend who's come over to bake a pie: *you might never go home*, she says.

---

45. This is just my theory; most people seem to assume it was Herb or one of the kids.

The book's portrayal of Bonnie makes more sense in the context of Capote's life and work. He had an intense and conflicted relationship with his own mother, who died young of alcoholism, and his early books are full of dead or absent mothers. He was drawn to women throughout his life, friends and allies he based characters on. In his first novel, *Other Voices, Other Rooms*, he transformed his old friend Harper Lee into Idabel Thompkins, an honor Lee would later reciprocate with Dill in *To Kill a Mockingbird*. The success of *Breakfast at Tiffany's* led to what Capote called "the Holly Golightly sweepstakes," in which various women claimed to be its heroine's inspiration. He would eventually lose many of his closest female friends because they felt betrayed by their portrayals in his work. Capote never met Bonnie Clutter, and some would say he betrayed her, anyway. But she's the best character in the book, besides her killer.

The Clutters didn't think so. Bonnie's younger brother was still outraged forty years later, when he granted his only interview on the subject. On the fiftieth anniversary of the murders, Diana Selsor Edwards, a cousin and childhood friend of Nancy Clutter's, wrote an essay for her tiny local newspaper in New Mexico calling Capote's portrayal "a great injustice," claiming he had turned her relatives into "cardboard figures."[46] The surviving Clutter daughters, both

---

46. It was later reprinted in the *Kansas City Star*, along with an interview in which Edwards describes the impetus for her essay: a few years earlier,

of whom still live in Kansas, claimed Capote had told them he was writing a "tribute" to their family and accused him of "grossly misrepresent[ing]" their parents and siblings for profit.[47] In 2017, two of Bonnie Clutter's granddaughters appeared in a documentary to dispute Capote's portrayal of her.[48] The family made a scrapbook to preserve their version of their murdered loved ones. But what good is a version of the story that nobody reads?

My copilot, Bonnie, shared a first name with Mrs. Clutter, and looked eerily like the pictures of her I'd seen on the internet:[49] warm, dark eyes, a sharp chin, big earrings and a winsome, off-kilter smile. Beyond those coincidences, Bonnie would probably object to any portrayal I give here. The objective version is that she was pale, pretty, sable-haired, five-seven, slender, had recently turned thirty. The less objective one is that we probably shouldn't have been dating

---

she was visiting the University of Arizona's photography center and saw a picture of the Clutter house, shot by Richard Avedon for *The New Yorker*, an experience she describes as "like getting hit with a baseball bat." Which means that her essay and this one originated on the same campus at the same time. See "Anniversary of *In Cold Blood* Killings Brings Memories from a Relative of the Clutter Family," November 13, 2009, A1.

47. Smith, Patrick. "Sisters, family: Surviving a legacy." From *Cold Blood: A Murder, a Book, a Legacy*, a 2005 University of Nebraska journalism project about the fortieth anniversary of Capote's book, 24. https://digitalcommons.unl.edu/journalismstudent/26.

48. Joe Berlinger's *Cold Blooded: The Clutter Family Murders*, a series on Sundance TV.

49. She disagrees with this.

at all. She was married to another man—she preferred to say separated—and she was a graduate student at the university where I taught, although I preferred to specify that she wasn't *my* student. Then there was the matter of her son, not yet three years old, who was back in Albuquerque, and himself another argument against us. I'd had my share of stepdads, the last of whom murdered my mother, and it was one of the things I swore I'd never be. I'd already become most of the others.

Bonnie had agreed to accompany me to a murder scene more readily than I expected. I don't know what the trip meant to her, but for me it was a pilgrimage of sorts. I'd been working on a book about my mother's murder, and writing about murder in America means living in the long shadow of *In Cold Blood*. I'd read Capote's book three times by then, had just taught it for the first time, and was finishing the final edits on a book inspired by it. I thought I knew everything there was to know about *In Cold Blood*. But all that knowledge somehow failed to warn me how much plans can change on trips to Kansas.

Earlier that day, it had happened to us. A few hours into the drive, the Rockies dropped us on the plains, like eggs onto a griddle, and what started as a spontaneous road trip turned into something else. She was driving fast, playing a Philip Glass album that sounded like two madmen fighting a piano duel; one song was inspired by "Wichita Sutra Vortex," an Allen Ginsberg poem he dictated into a tape recorder on a bus trip through Kansas the same year *In Cold Blood* came out. The poem reads like a companion piece, concerned with the same themes of a fractured American era: fear and lonesomeness, love and violence. But while Capote had faith in his own ability to render reality in prose, Ginsberg didn't believe writing could do it justice: *almost all our language has been taxed by war.* Ginsberg was heading west through Kansas, like Capote did. We were driving east, half a century later, in a different era with different wars, and I was starting to agree with Ginsberg.

On our timeless, horizontal drive to Holcomb, other cars became an event, a mystery of source and destination, and we wondered aloud who lived in those distant houses shrouded in trees, whether and how anyone could. We talked about time and technology, how we were piloting a dinosaur-powered vehicle across the floor of an ancient sea, what future civilizations would find here—all the insipid shit you can only say earnestly in a moment like that. Out the windows, fields rippled into the distance, and in that plane of wheat I saw the curvature of the earth. Our hands roamed lewdly as we drove. The past was lost in the apocalyptic flatness, along with the future, and the reasons we were there, and why we shouldn't do something doomed and stupid, like fall in love.

•

Despite what he would later claim, Capote didn't plan to write a book in Kansas. His original pitch was an article for *The New Yorker*. He told William Shawn, his editor there, that he wanted to write a piece about Holcomb's reaction to the killings, the fear and suspicion and collective sense of shock, a sleepy town in Middle America rocked by a gruesome act of violence. Capote had never written anything longer than a novella, and his new project had a narrow focus. When Capote arrived in Kansas, the first thing he said to Alvin Dewey, the Kansas Bureau of Investigation (KBI) agent in charge of the case, was that he didn't care if they caught the killers:[50] he wasn't there to write about *them*. He wanted the story to be about the victims, and what the murders did to their family, friends, and community. Capote couldn't have known what he was getting himself into, that his article would become a book that consumed the next six years of his life, and transformed the rest of it.

I sold my book four years before Bonnie and I went to Kansas, and my plans for it had changed considerably in the time since. Once I sat down to actually write the book, I realized I didn't know how. The pages I'd sent in the proposal were about the aftermath of my mother's death, a memoir

---

50. The comment did not go over well, although they later became close friends.

of my immediate grief, but my interest in that soon waned. A book about my mother's murder had to be about her, not me, and I didn't really know her, not well enough to portray permanently on the page, not after all those years of ignoring her memory and trying to move on. I had to find out who she really was.

I collected documents and photographs and home videos, found and talked to people who knew her before I did: her parents, ex-husbands, old friends. But the problem of portrayal persisted. The historical record didn't do justice to the mother I had known. I understood for the first time the inadequacy of fact, why the word first meant an action: something made, an evil deed.[51] Portraying a real person is always a harm done, an unforgivable and permanent reduction. That goes double for the dead, who are not the sum of the things they leave behind, or other people's memories. Something gets lost in their translation to the page, an intelligence, a sensibility, an essence. Their complexity. Their humanity.

I didn't know what to do about that, so I turned to invention. The first draft of my book included imagined vignettes in her perspective, private moments from her

---

51. It took forty years to morph into meaning something true, and that definition has remained, for centuries, a contradictory mess: *The Oxford English Dictionary*'s best guess is "that which is of the nature of a fact." (Second edition; it's the sixth meaning listed.)

life, events I knew had happened, more or less, but my interpretations of them. You could call those sections fiction, and others eventually would; I saw them as another kind of truth. Trying to portray my dead mother was, in its way, as hard as burying her. Writing a book about a murder changes your perspective, pulls back a veil. It made me feel differently about Capote in a few ways, one of which is a deep respect for the difficult work he did, even if I don't like the result.

Writing the book was one trial; publishing it was another. Bad omens arose almost immediately. I signed the contract in the pit of the 2008 financial crisis; a few days later, Random House laid off a large portion of its staff. My editor quit less than a year later, and my half-written book about losing a parent became what the industry calls an orphan, an irony I did not appreciate much. In what other writers would later tell me was an amateur move, I delivered the book on deadline. It met with months of silence. When I did hear back, they wanted me to cut all of the vignettes about my mother. I protested in the prideful way of a young and naive writer. (Capote had the same sort of disputes over his early books, notably *The Grass Harp*.) Someone raised the prospect of the book being rejected. My publisher had shrewdly paid me only part of the money up front, and that was long gone, spent on debt and book expenses and a few of the flourishes you might expect of a formerly poor person who comes into money, the same things Capote spent his first advance on: a sports car, a trip to Europe. I couldn't pay it back, even if I wanted to, and I didn't: I wanted the rest of the money. So I made most of the changes they asked for, hacked off a third of the book, and hoped that would be enough.

By the time we went to Holcomb, the publishing machine was almost done with me. Some writers like to compare their books to children. By then, I thought of mine more like a black-sheep uncle, the kind who shows up to the reunion on a motorcycle, gets drunk, and asks to borrow money. Nobody had seen Uncle Book for years, and people were starting to wonder if he might be dead. But the end was finally in sight: after being repeatedly pushed back, my publication date was eight months away.[52] A printed copy sat on the passenger floorboard of the car. The final edits were due in a week, and I'd been reading it out loud to Bonnie on the trip, listening for false notes. Other than my editor and agent, Bonnie was the book's first audience.

•

Like me, Capote didn't go to Kansas alone. He must have known the reception a man like him would get in rural Kansas. He was by all accounts a character: a miniature

---

52. It would later be pushed back another five months, for reasons I don't even want to discuss.

blond, bespectacled and handsome, but not in the waifish way of his youth, not by the time he went to Holcomb; his drug and alcohol habits were catching up with him, like a black car knifing through the Kansas night. Capote wore distinctive glasses, was fond of flowing scarves, and had a legendary voice, reedy and insinuating, one that would become a sort of trademark he seemed to embrace and even exaggerate at times, as if he was portraying himself the way he did the Clutters, by one defining characteristic.[53] But behind the act, Capote was deceptively tough,[54] cunning, and self-aware. He was also openly gay in a violently homophobic era, moreso in the Heartland. Capote attracted stares and crude comments everywhere he went in Kansas, and must have understood that, as an acquaintance of his put it, Holcombites "wouldn't be happy having this little gnome in his checkered vest running around asking questions about who'd murdered whom."[55] So he invited his childhood friend, Harper Lee, to come along.

---

53. He once wrote that his voice had "often been described as 'high and childish' (*among* other things)."

54. Clarke claims that Capote once beat Humphrey Bogart in an arm-wrestling match, and, in the ensuing scuffle, threw the reputed tough guy to the ground, breaking Bogart's arm.

55. This is John Barry Ryan, quoted in George Plimpton's unwieldily titled oral history *Truman Capote: In Which Various Friends, Enemies, Acquaintances, and Detractors Recall His Turbulent Career*, 168. Ryan also claims Capote asked Lee to bring a gun and carry it with her while they were there.

Lee had been friends with Capote since before that was his name.[56] She was his childhood neighbor in Monroeville, Alabama, and followed him to New York with the same dream to be an author. When he invited her to Kansas, she had recently finished *To Kill a Mockingbird*, in which she had immortalized her old friend as the thinly disguised Dill.[57] Lee was awaiting her book's publication, and probably needed a distraction, so she agreed to go.[58] Months after completing one immortal American book, Harper Lee helped write another.

Lee took copious notes—she typed up more than 150 pages for Capote's use—and did much of the reporting and interviewing. But her most important contribution was probably to grease the skids for her old friend. Lee was a warm and charming woman, and performed her Southernness in a way Capote rarely allowed himself to; she fit in with the locals in a way he decidedly did not. Bobby

56. He was born Truman Parsons, and later took the last name of his step-father, Joe Capote.
57. I haven't been able to figure out how Capote felt about this: he mentions it occasionally in his writing, in an opaque and evenhanded way. He and Lee drifted apart after they returned from Kansas, a chill that's often attributed to the success of their respective books. I wonder if it also had to do with how she wrote him as a character, in a book that became an American classic. Maybe he learned how Holcombites felt.
58. He paid her $900, and she wasn't his first choice—first Capote invited his friend, Andrew Lyndon, but he refused. This is from *Casey Cep's Furious Hours: Murder, Fraud, and the Last Trial of Harper Lee*. Knopf, 2019, 180–81.

Rupp, Nancy Clutter's boyfriend and the last person to see the family alive, said that if Lee hadn't been there when he was interviewed, he would've walked out of the room.[59] Lee made such a good impression that a local couple invited them to Christmas dinner, which opened up the town's society to the two outsiders. Despite those contributions, Capote never gave her proper credit. He would later dedicate *In Cold Blood* partly to Lee, but he referred to her only once in the book, as "a woman reporter,"[60] and later called her his "assistant researchist." After Kansas, their friendship would never be the same.

A lot of things wouldn't. Five weeks into their stay, Capote and Lee joined a crowd outside the Garden City courthouse, where the accused killers of the Clutter family were soon to arrive. By then, Capote thought he had what he needed for the story. He'd finagled his way into the town's good graces, and had befriended Alvin Dewey, the man in charge of the investigation. He and Lee had learned all the details, read all the reports, talked to nearly everyone in Holcomb. They were almost ready to return to New York when they went to dinner at the Deweys' one night and the

---

59. See Ralph F. Voss's *Truman Capote and the Legacy of In Cold Blood*. Tuscaloosa: University of Alabama Press, 2011, 195.
60. This mention, in which the reporter talks to Hickock's mother in the women's bathroom, doesn't definitely refer to Lee, but she seems like the most likely candidate.

phone rang during the meal: the killers had been caught in Las Vegas. Dewey drove out to pick them up—a snowstorm forced him to spend a night in Albuquerque—and brought them back to the Finney County courthouse. Capote and Lee waited on the courthouse steps to see the killers.

Capote would later write the scene through the eyes of two stray cats, a peculiar choice for a book of nonfiction. Silence falls over the shivering crowd as a convoy of police cars pulls up to the curb, and the two suspects take their perp walk up the stairs, blinking in the camera flash. The cats don't record Capote's reaction when he first saw Perry Smith, diminutive, doe-eyed and brooding—there but for the grace of god went Truman. That moment changed everything: Capote's book, his career, his life, the future of American nonfiction. Lee called it "the beginning of a great love affair."[61]

•

Bonnie and I didn't have directions to River Valley Farm, the former home of the Clutter family, and our phones had long since lost service in the wastelands of west Kansas. We crept the streets of Holcomb in our borrowed silver

61. This is quoted in multiple sources, probably first in Clarke, 326. She said it at the arraignment, not on the courthouse steps, but the sentiment applies.

Saturn, looking for a treelined driveway matching Capote's description, or what I remembered of it. It didn't take long to find it, but I'll save you the trouble: take old Route 50 east through town, go south on Main, west on Oak, follow it to the end.

We stopped at the mouth of the driveway, staring at the farm, the elms, the barns and fields, the handsome white house in the distance, wrapped in a browning lawn. In 1959, it was the kind of place that signified wealth. Smith claims in the book that when the killers reached this spot, Hickock said, "Look at this spread! Don't tell me this guy ain't loaded." Smith agreed, but something about the atmosphere bothered him: "it was sort of *too* impressive."[62]

Not anymore. All that irrigated wheat had slowly sucked the aquifer dry, and drought did a number on the elms, which were all dead or dying or stumps. Still, it was easy to see how the Clutter driveway might once have been foreboding, a tunnel under the overhanging limbs, like staring down a barrel. A metal gate across the entrance hung open, but a handpainted, pink-lettered sign prohibited trespassing; it was the kind of incongruous detail Capote would have loved. We parked across the street, got out of the car, and stood in a searing wind, wiping dust from our eyes, staring across a wheat field at the house half-hidden by a shelterbelt.

---

62. Ibid., 235.

The critic Ralph F. Voss devotes a chapter of his estimable book about *In Cold Blood* to how it reflects the Southern gothic style, including its emphasis on houses as scenes of hidden violence and hauntings. He mentions *To Kill a Mockingbird* as arguably the most popular example— the gray, ramshackle Radley Place—and Lee was the one who recorded most of the details on which Capote based his portrait of the Clutter house.[63] My own pet theory is that Capote also drew from *Psycho*, Hitchcock's pioneering slasher film,[64] which came out the year after he first went to Holcomb; it was hard to look out at the Clutter house in the distance and not think of the Bates mansion, the archetype of American murder scenes. But that was a tourist's point of view. If I hadn't read the book, it might have looked like any other Kansas farmhouse with a brown and patchy lawn.

As we drove back down Oak, three men we'd passed earlier were still slouched against the bedsides of a Chevy truck, tilting bottles of beer and watching us. The biggest walked out into the road and raised a hand. I stopped and rolled down the window. He shielded his eyes against the dust and spoke: "You got no brake lights."

"Stay here," I said to Bonnie. I got out of the car and

63. See Cep's book for more on this.
64. Or the Robert Bloch novel of the same name, which came out a few months before Capote went to Kansas, and is based on the real-life serial killer Ed Gein.

followed the Samaritan around back. I was taller than him, but his torso was as broad as a small bear's, his boots grimy in the way I imagined farmers' were. His two friends stayed by the truck, watching, a shifty-eyed teenager and an old man who could've been whittled from a twig. I called to Bonnie, asking her to hit the brakes. I meant for her to reach over and press the pedal, but I didn't say that, and she got out of the car, big sunglasses and a little black shirt and cutoffs that clung to her ass, looking hotter than the wind drying the sweat off of my ribs. As the men watched her, I thought fleetingly of two others driving down this street, all those years ago, breaking into that house at the end of the lane, not getting what they wanted.

The brake lights didn't work. I let out a breath I hadn't known I was holding, and remembered enough of my old self to engage in a working-class male conversation: it was probably a fuse, maybe a relay; the other lights worked, so it couldn't be anything worse. The big guy mentioned an Auto Zone in Garden, a little while down the road. I thanked him, and had my hand on the car door, thinking we were out of the woods, when he said he'd seen me taking pictures.

I stopped, paused, turned to face him. He stood in the middle of the street, thumbs in his belt loops, legs wide as a gunfighter's.

"We're just passing through." It seemed like the thing to say, a line remembered from an old script, what the stranger in town tells the sheriff. I tried to shut myself up, but out it came: "I'm a big fan of the book."

The teenager, swear to God, spat into the dirt. The old man's squint clamped down a little more. I remembered from something I'd read that Bobby Rupp still lived in Holcomb; he would've been about the right age. The Samaritan jerked a meaty hand over his shoulder, toward the Clutter farm. "You can go on up the driveway if you want."

I shook my head, spread my hands. "Don't want to bother nobody." The grammar of the rural poor sounded condescending, even though it once was mine.

"Nobody to bother," he said. "I'm right here."

"You live there?"

"Yep." His rough hand gripped mine, not nearly as hard as I'd expected, and he said his name was Brian. "This happens all the time."

In that moment, I wanted nothing more than to get the hell out of Kansas, but we turned the car around and drove slowly back down the street, through the gate, beneath the elms.

•

In Cold Blood works by withholding: Capote avoids the murder itself until a little more than halfway through, textbook timing for a tragic climax. Almost two hundred pages after our last glimpse of the Clutters, the book finally gives us its only account of the murders, from the killer's point of view, when Smith confesses in the backseat of a police cruiser somewhere in Arizona. It's probably the most important passage in the book, because it answers the question readers want to know, even if we don't admit it: how does it feel to kill someone?

In Cold Blood tells us exactly that, in the murderer's words. In Smith's version, he and Hickock break into the house, wake up the Clutters, lock them in the bathroom, and search for the safe full of money an old cellmate told them about. Instead, they find forty dollars, a radio, and a pair of binoculars. Smith takes their haul outside, puts it in the car, and stands for a moment in the driveway, looking up at the moon, savoring the November chill. He thinks about leaving, walking to the highway, hitching a ride. But he can't. "It was like I wasn't part of it," Smith says in his confession. "More as though I was reading a story. And I had to know what was going to happen. The end." So he goes inside and slits Herb Clutter's throat. Months later, in the backseat of the car, he claims he didn't mean to do it: "I didn't realize what I'd done till I heard the sound."

Smith never said that. A reporter named Philip K. Tompkins went to Kansas after *In Cold Blood*'s release to investigate its accuracy. He found transcripts of the confession itself and reports by the detectives who were in the car. Only in the book does Smith express regret. "To judge from his confession," Tompkins writes, "Perry Smith was an obscene, semi-literate, and cold-blooded killer."[65]

In Capote's version, Smith is eloquent, reluctant, full of regret, almost humane. After cutting Mr. Clutter's throat, he shoots the struggling man to put him out of his misery. He places a pillow under Kenyon's head before he nearly blows it off. He spares Nancy from his partner's intended rape before they kill her, too. By the time the killers walk down the hall to Bonnie's room, Capote has the victim asking for it: "Perhaps, having heard all she had, Bonnie welcomed their swift approach."[66]

Perhaps not. Capote didn't seem to mind speculating, speaking for the Clutters and calling it all true, "immaculately factual."[67] But there's no way of knowing what they felt in their last moments alive, no way to portray them accurately. Murder erases the victims, leaving only a vast, annihalating silence. To write about a murder is to confront the limits of human of knowledge, the impossibility of portrayal, the mystery of death itself.

It's no wonder Capote decided to focus on the killer instead. Smith was still alive at the time, available to him, a mystery he could solve. In his biography of Capote, Gerald

---

65. "In Cold Fact," *Esquire*, June 1966.
66. Capote, 245.
67. This is from Plimpton's *New York Times* interview.

Clarke remarks on the "many unsettling similarities" between the author and his protagonist: they had similar childhoods, both raised in broken homes, and grew up as stunted, rootless outsiders, boyish, sensitive, artistic. Capote saw himself in Smith, and found that irresistible, artistically and perhaps romantically—a KBI agent later implied they may have had hallway trysts on death row.[68] So Capote took a man others described as a dwarfish sociopath and portrayed him as a frustrated and mistreated dreamer, a guitar-strumming poet prone to fantasies of Mexican treasure and a big yellow bird that protected him in his sleep,[69] a murderous Peter Pan. The Perry Smith of *In Cold Blood* resembles the protagonists of Capote's previous work: Joel Knox of *Other Voices, Other Rooms*; Collin Fenwick of *The Grass Harp*.[70] John Knowles, who was close with Capote, called his protagonists "special, strange gifted people [who] have to be treated with understanding."[71] *In Cold Blood* takes a thirty-one-year-old professional felon of no particular account and makes him into what Norman Mailer called one of the great characters

---

68. Harold Nye, quoted in Plimpton's oral history, 188–89. This seems like a dubious assertion: Nye disliked Capote, and he admits he can't prove it. Nye also, perhaps more credibly, claimed Capote fictionalized parts of the book that featured him: "It was a fiction book," he said. (175.).

69. The critic Sol Yurick pointed out that Capote may have "lifted" the parrot from Flaubert, one of the latter's favorite writers. See Voss, 60.

70. A number of critics have made this observation. See Voss, 77, for an overview.

71. Plimpton, 175.

of American literature.[72]

People who knew Perry Smith—the detectives, fellow convicts, his sister, even Hickock, his partner in crime—spoke of him with contempt or fear. Alvin Dewey, who took Smith's confession, described him as a stone-cold killer. Almost everyone who met the two murderers preferred Hickock. Everyone but Capote. *In Cold Blood* devotes more than one hundred pages to portraying Perry Smith, more than twice the space it gives the Clutters. It quotes, at excessive length, an autobiographical narrative Smith wrote for a court psychiatrist, a similar account by his father, and letters from his sister, among other sources. It gives Smith's account of his childhood and his supposed hesitance to kill, reveals the extravagant self-pity of his letters from jail. From the beginning, Capote conceived of the book as a tragedy: hence the grain elevators rising like Greek temples, the minor Holcombites who serve as a chorus, its classical story arc and emphasis on fate. Hickock is the second actor, the police and justice system the antagonists, the victims mere vehicles for the hero's hamartia. The hero is Perry Smith.

•

We emerged from the ravaged elms into a clearing and

72. Clarke, 315.

stopped where the killers must have. I tried to imagine Smith standing here that night, staring at the moon, debating whether to leave. To our left stood a silo, a barn, and a mobile home with the wheels still on; to the right, the Clutter house. It still looked like Capote's description of it, although he was imprecise: he calls it a white house, but the first story is pale yellow brick. It had been updated some over the years, with new siding and a split-log fence, a satellite dish perched on the steep angle of a red-shingled roof. Herb Clutter designed the house himself, and oversaw its construction, during which he made an offhand comment to one of his employees about having paid ten thousand dollars for lumber.[73] Ten years later, that employee, Floyd Wells, wound up prison cellmates with Dick Hickock; somehow the Clutter farm came up, and Wells misremembered a safe full of money. So, in one version of the story, the house was what got the Clutters killed.

For reasons I can't explain, Capote omitted the detail about the lumber payment from *In Cold Blood*.[74] Maybe it was a question of selection: he wanted the story to start not with a house, or with Wells, or even with Hickock, but with Perry Smith. To Capote—and to us—the house was relevant only as a setting for four murders, and his gothic descriptions of it focused on the elms, the wind, the

---

73. This info is taken from *Cold Blooded*, Episode 1.
74. Wells' statement is part of the KBI files, which he had access to, so I'm assuming he knew about it.

bloodstains on the walls, its ghostly silence afterward.

The Samaritan had warned us not to get out of the car because of a dog, another coincidence that seemed to collapse time. Mr. Clutter had a dog, a "part-collie mongrel" Capote mentions but doesn't name. Later in the book, during Perry Smith's confession, Alvin Dewey asks about the dog, says they couldn't figure out why it didn't bark, and Smith says he didn't see any dog. Neither did we. We sat there in the car, looking at a house where four people we never met were murdered before we were born. It reminded me of my childhood in Tombstone, mocking the tourists lining up to see the O.K. Corral, where three men were shot dead a century ago, and now throngs of Midwesterners and Germans mill around the effigies, wondering why they traveled all that way to see an alley by the highway.

Back on Oak, the men were where we'd left them, and what had been strange now seemed sinister, their watching, our trips up and down the street, this absurd ritual of seeing the house. I slowed the car to a crawl, cracked my window, yelled a thanks. The Samaritan nodded, pointed to the beer in his hand, cocked an eyebrow. I shook my head and kept going.

"I couldn't tell if they hated us," Bonnie said.

"Me neither," I said, but I was lying. They hated us.

Later I would read on the Internet that the big guy's name was spelled Bryan, and that his parents, who knew the

Clutters, bought the house for a dollar[75] because of its history. After the murders, it stood empty for months, and was used as a set for the movie adaptation of *In Cold Blood.* The couple who bought it stayed only a year, for reasons that were not recorded, and the next owner killed himself. Bryan's parents moved in thirty years after the murders. The visits started while they were still unpacking. They'd tried everything, multiple times a day, all hours of the night, morbid book pilgrims from all over the world driving up the lane, taking pictures of the house. Supposedly Bryan used to shoot guns in the air to scare them off. They put up a gate, installed a sign. When none of that worked, they tried giving tours for five dollars, but the neighbors got upset. Six years before we showed up, the owners listed the house at auction, with the condition that whoever bought it couldn't sensationalize or exploit it.[76] The open house drew tourists from great distances, some of whom wanted to see the basement wall still supposedly stained with Herb Clutter's blood, but the auction didn't draw a satisfactory bid. As I write this, they're about to list it for sale again; the agent's mother was friends

---

75. They also paid "other valuable consideration." See Wiebe, Crystal K. "In the End, Just a Home." *Lawrence Journal-World*, 4/6/2005: https://www2.ljworld.com/news/2005/apr/06/in_the_end.

76. Campbell, Matt. "Lenexa Man Has Rare Photos Inside 'In Cold Blood' House Where Kansas Family Was Slain." *The Kansas City Star*, November 22, 2017. https://www.kansascity.com/news/local/crime/article185886788.html.

with Nancy Clutter.[77] Bryan's father once called it one of the most famous houses in America. His mother once said she wanted to burn it. After Capote finagled his way inside the Clutter house and described it to the world, the surviving family wished they would've torn it down.[78]

I doubt it would've made a difference. While I was writing my book, I went back to the place where my mother died, a trailer way out in the desert, the exact middle of nowhere, and found all trace of her erased. It didn't make me feel any better.

•

In Cold Blood never says who killed the Clutters. At first, Smith claimed he and Hickock each killed two of them. Smith would later change his testimony, admitting to all four murders. Alvin Dewey said Smith only changed his story so that Hickock's mother wouldn't have to live with knowing her son was a murderer; the detective believed to the end that Smith's original confession was true. Capote disagreed: he thought Smith killed all of the Clutters. The book suggests the same, but leaves the question unanswered.

77. Trapasso, Clare. "The Untold Story Behind the Infamous 'In Cold Blood' Murder House—and Why It's for Sale." Realtor. com, October 24, 2019. https://www.realtor.com/news/trends/in-cold-blood-murder-house-for-sale.
78. A granddaughter says as much in *Cold Blooded*, Episode 2.

It must not have seemed important.

Capote was more concerned with another question: why? Like all the greats, he understood aspects of American culture that we don't admit, to others or to ourselves, dark inclinations only obvious in the stories we tell and consume. We care more about killers than we do about victims, and more about why they do it than we do about the murders themselves. Motive suggests a logic, and if murder conforms to logic, we can believe it won't happen to us, even in one of the most murderous countries in the world, one where it happens to forty-four people every day.[79] *In Cold Blood* reassures its readers: if we understand *why* people commit murder, we can avoid it. It also suggests a dark and prevalent American logic: if the Clutters were murdered, they must have done something to deserve it.

Capote spends more of the book trying to answer why Smith killed the Clutters than he devotes to the murders themselves. While Smith is holed up in a Garden City prison cell, awaiting trial, he tells a visiting friend that he did kill them all, and that he doesn't know why. "It wasn't because of anything the Clutters did," he says. "They never hurt me. Like other people. Like people have all my life. Maybe it's just that the Clutters were the ones who had to pay for it."[80] He says he's not sorry, that it doesn't bother him a bit. He says it was

---

79. As of 2018.
80. Capote, 290.

easy, "like picking off targets in a shooting gallery." The scene's accuracy is suspect: Capote wasn't there, and there's too much dialogue, too much detail, for it to have been recreated from interviews. He uses Perry Smith to make the book's main theme explicit: "The good people of Kansas want to murder me," Smith says. "And some hangman will be glad to get the work." Like the book as a whole, the passage begins as the story of the Clutter murders and becomes an argument against capital punishment instead.

Smith never gave a reason for the killings, not a real one, just maybes and self-pity. So Capote found one himself. During the trial, the defense claimed temporary insanity, and called a psychiatrist, Dr. W. Mitchell Jones, to testify on the mental state of the killers. His actual testimony was restricted by Kansas law to saying whether the killers knew right from wrong at the time of the murder, a precedent based on the M'Naghton rule, a law Capote describes, not very objectively, as "an ancient British importation which contends that if the accused knew the nature of his act, and knew it was wrong, then he is mentally competent and responsible for his actions."[81] On the stand, Dr. Jones said that Hickock did know right from wrong, and that he didn't have an opinion on Perry Smith. When the defense attorney asked him to

---

81. 267. That description isn't quite accurate, either. The M'Naghten rule originated in 1843, and it's hardly as arcane as that phrasing suggests: more than half of US states still use some form of it.

explain, the prosecution objected and prevented him from saying any more.

In the book, though, Capote goes on to tell us what Dr. Jones *would* have said, a sly, hypothetical scene he sneaks into the real one. Dr. Jones claims that Perry Smith shows signs of severe mental illness: paranoia, rage, and other symptoms of a possible thought disorder or "mental abnormality"; Jones says he'd need to evaluate Smith more to be certain, but calls his personality "very nearly that of a paranoid schizophrenic."

After including a diagnosis that was never given in court, Capote leaves the scene of the trial entirely to consult another psychiatrist, Dr. Joseph Satten. The book spends almost five pages quoting at length an article Satten co-authored on "murder without apparent motive," which argues for a category of killer somewhere between sane and insane, one who kills senselessly in a dissociative state. Satten claims that Smith fits the profile, and may have killed Herb Clutter "under a mental eclipse, deep inside a schizophrenic darkness." Mr. Clutter represented everyone who'd ever wronged him: his father, the orphanage nuns who abused him, the military, the justice system, the unnamed "they" he raged constantly against. Smith saw his pain and alienation writ large in his victims, a conventional Kansas family. The book attributes all of that to Satten, but the passage sounds suspiciously like Capote's opinion. Weeks after the book's release, Capote would admit in an interview that Satten never talked to Smith, and that he himself believed Perry didn't mean to kill the Clutters, but had "a brain explosion."[82] But because Capote left himself out of the book, he had to make other characters a mouthpiece for that view: Dr. Satten, Smith. *I didn't realize what I'd done till I heard the sound.*

Smith's confession suggests the murders were at least partly a rational decision: before killing the Clutters, he and Hickock discussed their options and the likely outcomes. He also says he might have done it because he was mad at his partner, for being wrong about the safe, and for wanting to rape a teenage girl. *In Cold Blood* ignores those explanations, and suggests, like the tragedies it's modeled on, that it was Smith's destiny to kill, because he had a traumatic childhood full of abuse and divorce and neglect. But so did Capote, and he never killed anyone.[83] So did I, and I haven't killed anyone, either.

•

The sun was setting and our brake lights didn't work, and we

---

82. Plimpton, George. "The Story Behind a Nonfiction Novel." *New York Times*, January 16, 1966, https://archive.nytimes.com/www.nytimes.com/books/97/12/28/home/capote-interview.html.

83. Not directly, at least, although another of his portrayals, many years later, would lead to its subject's suicide.

had six more hours to drive down a dark highway, so I stopped the car outside the old Holcomb School, where the Clutter children went, and kneeled on the hot asphalt, peering into the fusebox under the dashboard. I didn't know which fuse did what and I didn't have the owner's manual and it wasn't my car, so I yanked the fuses one by one, and everything turned on and off—the radio, the blinkers—but the brake lights refused to kindle, and as the pavement began to cook my knees, déjá vu set in. I'd never been to Kansas before that I could recall, certainly not with another man's wife in another man's car, and I thought it felt familiar because that's the kind of situation I get myself into, the kind that's hard to explain, until I remembered where I'd seen this street before: on the cover of my worn paperback copy of *In Cold Blood*. I'd recently lent it to Bonnie. She hadn't read the book, and I think she wanted to see what I was so obsessed with before we came to Kansas. Our relationship was new, and we were trying to understand each other. We still thought we could.

I didn't understand my own obsession with the book. I'd read *In Cold Blood* a few times by then, growing angrier with each read at its moral project, the glorification of a homicidal halfwit, and more outraged by its endless legacy: it made focusing on the murderer the default mode of murder stories, laid a cornerstone of killer worship in American culture. But what right did I have to be outraged? Here I was, in Holcomb, Kansas, seeing the murder sites, and right there on the floorboard, under the fuses I'd flung in annoyance, sat my own murder book. I had told myself my story was different, that I was honoring my mother and my book would serve some great purpose, that it might help call attention to the epidemic of domestic violence in America. I thought I'd written a murder story that did what Capote originally intended: focused on the victim, their family, the community. But my name was on the checks, and my name would be on the cover soon, and the writing was on the wall already, before I'd even finished the copy edits, easier to read with each pushed-back publication date, every desultory email from my publisher. My book would never be as successful as *In Cold Blood*, and it wouldn't do anything to change the cultural conversation about murder. Nobody wants to read about a victim, because it forces us to imagine being one. And what good is a response nobody reads?

Before the trip, I hadn't read my book in a long time. I'd written and revised it in pieces, losing track of the whole, until it began to feel like a maze built by a lost version of myself, one I was stuck inside. In the years I'd spent on it, I'd learned why writers compare their books to raising children, building houses, climbing mountains: you can't see what it is until you're done. Only earlier that day, somewhere west of where we were, reading to Bonnie my own words about a dead woman she would never meet, had I finally under-stood what I'd done, and felt the weight of it. Readers would know my mother only from my portrayal. What a thing to do to the dead, what an act of hubris: to preserve your version of them forever, a portrait in amber, one they can't dispute. The same thing Capote did to the Clutters.

I couldn't get the lights to work. We sat in the car, sweating, discussing what to do. Our plan had been to visit the Clutter grave in Garden City. That seemed absurd now that we'd seen the house, but we continued, caught up in its dumb inertia, as if we, too, were characters in a story: we had to know what would happen, the end.

I drove to the AutoZone in Garden City the Samaritan had suggested, where I scraped a dead bird out of the Saturn's grille—where were Capote's cats when you needed them?—and bought a new fuse that didn't fix the brake lights. Before we left, I asked the clerk where the graveyard was. He asked which one I meant. I couldn't remember the name, and we'd forgotten the book, so I said the one with all the trees. He gave me the look I deserved, and directions to the closest cemetery.

It was the wrong one, an eerie, treeless square deleted from the wheat, like an experimental plot for growing granite. Bonnie got a miraculous bar of service and searched on her phone for nearby cemeteries while I watched the setting sun reveal the hidden textures in the land around us, shadow fingers stretching out from tombstones. Bonnie finally announced triumphantly that she had found it, said it wasn't far, told me which way to go. She'd grown invested in our morbid little tour. Maybe I'd picked the perfect companion, after all: a poet prone to finding romance in unexpected places, like graveyards where mismatched lovers search for murdered strangers. A few highway ramps and we were there, at Valley View. I was glad to see that at least one place still looked like Capote had described it, an oasis of trees and grass amid the wheat, "a good refuge from a hot day." As far as I had seen it was the greenest place in Kansas. We parked in the shade and went looking for the Clutters.

•

Capote didn't just embellish; he also left out some salient facts. In an interview with George Plimpton after the book came out, Capote called writing nonfiction a question of selection, and used a botanical analogy: if the entire story of the murders was a plant, his book reduced it to a seed.[84] (Judging by its legacy, he was right, although perhaps not in the way he intended.) He said a nonfiction author shouldn't appear in the work, so as not to intrude, but could guide the reader by what he chose to tell: they could manipulate characters, for instance, and comment on the story by setting it "in a context of qualification."

One of Capote's qualifications was omitting a possible

---

84. Plimpton, George. "The Story Behind a Nonfiction Novel."

motive for the murders. Voss devotes a chapter of his critical study of *In Cold Blood* to its gay subtext, which was noted by some critics after its publication, but overshadowed, then as now, by the brouhaha over Capote's use of the term "nonfiction novel." Plimpton asked Capote if the killers had a sexual relationship, and he denied it, saying that Hickock was "aggressively heterosexual" and Smith's "sexual interests were practically nil." But Voss points out a number of facts that cast doubt on Capote's claim. The killers were former cellmates; Perry is repeatedly referred to as a "punk," a coeval prison slur for gay men, and described in feminine terms; he rarely shows interest in women, and seems jealous of Hickock's liaisons with them. Hickock also calls Smith pet names throughout the book, such as "honey" and "sugar" and "baby." At one point, they "pick up" a German lawyer and his male companion in an Acapulco bar and spend days boating with them; when the German gives Smith his sketchbook as a parting gift, it contains "nude studies" of Hickock. The killers also share hotel rooms all over America and Mexico, staying together for months after the crime, long after they have any apparent reason to. Their homosexuality remains a subtext only because Capote refuses to acknowledge it.

Capote knew his readership. His books sold well, and usually made bestseller lists. He had seen his early books criticized for portraying homosexuality,[85] and was savvy enough to know that if he wanted *In Cold Blood* to make him the most famous writer in America, as it soon would, it had to cater to the mainstream American sensibilities of the mid-sixties; in other words, having a gay protagonist would cripple the book's commercial prospects. (The same audience had no qualms about murdering protagonists, or depictions of graphic violence; Robert Bloch's novel *Psycho*, and Hitchcock's film adaptation, had proven that a few years earlier.) So Capote left out Smith and Hickock's sexual relationship. It was probably a smart decision: the killers' sexuality shouldn't make a difference, and omitting it likely avoided a lot of homophobic vitriol.

But what if it was relevant? In his confession—or at least in Capote's version of it—Smith stops Hickock from raping Nancy Clutter because he was disgusted, and despised anyone who couldn't "control themselves sexually." Later, right before he cuts Herb Clutter's throat, Smith says, as a cryptic explanation, "It was something between me and Dick." Voss proposes that something was jealousy, that Smith's sense of rejection led him to kill, which would explain what he calls "one of the great ironies within *In Cold Blood*": moments after sparing Nancy from rape, Smith murders her father, sealing the fate of the entire family.[86] In

---

85. Among many examples, his former editor and mentor, George Davis, called *Other Voices, Other Rooms* "the fairy Huckleberry Finn," a response that wounded Capote deeply. See Clarke, 158.

Voss's version, the story of the Clutter murders becomes a different kind of tragedy, more Shakespeare than Sophocles, less about fate than it is about love: betrayal, jealous rage, the consequences of one catastrophic choice.

Capote might argue that even the motive for the murders was a matter of selection. He had no obligation to outline every possible reason Smith may have killed the Clutters, and doing so would have bogged down the book. And maybe it doesn't matter why he did it, only that he did; as I'd discovered writing my own book about murder, you can never answer the question of why. But Capote spends a hundred pages on Smith's sordid past, all the wrongs that had been done to him, and finally puts an explanation in his character's mouth, words he never said. The book makes it seem like Smith didn't mean to do it, almost as if it wasn't his fault. Maybe that doesn't matter, either; in the days after my mother's murder, when we didn't yet know who'd done it, I was surprised by how little I considered that question. Even if we found out who did it, and why, and how, it wouldn't change anything: she'd still be dead. And if the story wasn't for the victims, and it wasn't their families, who was it for?

•

86. The quote is from page 117. This passage paraphrases Voss's scenario, which occupies pages 114–18.

Valley View Cemetery was windless and calm, dappled by sunlight slanting through the trees. At a junction in the path, Bonnie spotted the grave of Alvin Dewey, flanked by his wife and father. He died in 1987, a few years after Capote, his unlikely friend, who had often hosted him and his wife in New York, introducing them to the aristocracy and inviting them to his blockbuster Black & White ball.[87]

In Cold Blood ends with Dewey's point of view. The passage begins with the hangings. Capote dispatches Hickock in the space of a few sentences. After his body is taken away, Smith walks into the warehouse, and the book's two heroes meet for the last time. Smith spots Dewey in the crowd, grins and winks at him, then climbs the gallows, stares out at the gathered crowd, says he doesn't believe in capital punishment, and apologizes for his crimes. The executioner puts the mask over Smith's head, and Dewey shuts his eyes. He keeps them shut as he hears the snap, remembering the first time he saw Smith, "the dwarfish boy-man," sitting in an interrogation room, feet not touching the floor. When Dewey opens his eyes, he sees "the same childish feet, tilted, dangling."[88] Later, Dewey said he never closed his eyes.[89]

---

87. Duane West, the prosecuting attorney in the Clutter case, claimed that Capote and Dewey's friendship distorted the book. He said Capote exaggerated Dewey's role in catching the killers, and West objected to the book's sympathetic portrayal of the killers: "The whole thing was garbage," he said. Quoted in Plimpton's oral history, 224.

Dewey would call the Clutter case the biggest of his career, but not the hardest: the detective saw the story as much more straightforward than the author did, a tale of two common criminals botching a robbery, slaughtering a family in cold blood, and getting the punishment they deserved. Dewey believed Smith's confession, and wasn't especially fascinated with him, or sad to see him hang.

Capote was the one who felt guilty. As the killers awaited execution, Capote claimed to be excited at the prospect. At those New York parties, talking about his book, he told whoever would listen that he could hardly wait for the hanging; when the last appeal failed, he said he was beside himself with joy.[90] But when the time came, Capote almost didn't attend, and he refused to answer Smith's phone calls the day of the hangings.[91] But he did finally go to the warehouse, out of a sense of duty to his friend, and when Smith didn't have the decency to apologize for what he'd done, Capote invented one. None of the other reporters in the room, taking notes as the condemned man spoke, recorded or remembered it—only Capote, who some witnesses claimed had left the room by then, unable to watch. A fake confession hadn't been enough:

---

88. Capote, 341.

89. Plimpton, 187.

90. Plimpton, 215–16. His audience didn't buy it; one said he was "clearly in love with" Smith.

91. He tried to avoid the previous execution date by staying in Europe. See Clarke, 353–54.

he invented an apology, too. And still he wasn't done. After the executions, when he could finally finish the last section of *In Cold Blood*, he wrote it as a treatise against capital punishment. He needed a mouthpiece for his views, so he chose his friend Dewey. But the detective wasn't thinking about poor Perry Smith as he hung: after seeing the way Nancy Clutter looked, he said, he could've pulled the lever himself.[92]

As I stood over Dewey,'s grave Bonnie called me over to a nearby plot: she'd found the Clutters. *In Cold Blood* ends at the Clutter grave. Capote writes that the four victims share a single stone, "in a far corner of the cemetery—beyond the trees, out in the sun, almost at the wheat field's bright edge."[93] If that had ever been true, it wasn't anymore. A cypress draped the grave in shade, and stones stretched for fifty yards in every direction. Herb and Bonnie were buried together under one marker, the children beneath smaller satellites on each side, all three stones tinting pink in the dusk. Pinwheels spun on the kids' graves, plastic flowers for the parents.

In the closing pages of the book, Dewey finishes weeding his father's plot and walks over to pay his respects to the Clutters. At their grave, he finds Susan Kidwell, a friend of Nancy's who discovered her body the morning after the murders. They chat briefly about how much has

92. Plimpton, 187.
93. Capote, 342.

changed since that terrible day, and afterward, Dewey walks out beneath the trees, "leaving behind him the big sky, the whisper of wind voices in the wind-bent wheat."[94] The last line always rang false to me, its tinge of melodrama, the gothic personification and sloppy second "wind," Capote's penchant for alliteration left unchecked. Maybe that's because it was: the whole last scene is fiction.

Capote selected facts, left out others, fabricated so many parts of the book. He denied all of it, claiming that every word was true. Even Clarke's biography—which was, somewhat ironically, authorized by Capote—makes the delusional claim that nobody "unearthed any errors of substance" in *In Cold Blood*.[95] The one major exception, the one lie Capote himself acknowledged,[96] was the ending. Capote couldn't bring himself to end with the hangings, a passage supposedly so difficult to write that it paralyzed his hand: he said he wanted "to bring everything back full circle, to end with peace."[97] After all those pages about the killer, his bleak childhood and thwarted ambitions, his plight on death row, Capote couldn't end with Smith's dead feet dangling from the gallows. Instead he leaves us with a gesture to the victims, a sentimental scene that never happened, one final

---

94. Ibid., 343.
95. Clarke, *Capote*, 358..
96. Ibid., 358-59.
97. Ibid., 359.

look at their resting place. A false apology of his own.

Crossing the graveyard on the way back to the car, I told Bonnie I felt like a tourist. "Maybe it's good to be remembered," she said, and I wondered how a person could be so unapologetically herself. We talked about what we'd want done with us after we died, funerals and music and epitaphs, and how we might need to decide soon, because we were about to drive halfway across Kansas with no brake lights. It was a joke, but I thought about it: we could die out on that highway, wind up buried in some place like this, leave our story to someone else's telling.

As I got into the car, I accidentally stepped on my book, and a few pages scattered across the footwell. I picked them up. They were the last scene, the moment of my mother's murder, her last few seconds alive. It's told in third person, no narrator, no *I*; it goes deep into her mind, her dreams and memories. I had no way of knowing what she thought, knowing she was about to die, so I imagined it. It was my version, based on what I knew of her. I'd justified writing it by telling myself that I knew her better than anyone else alive, and that was true. But my ending fit my own selfish agenda: in my book, her last thoughts were of me. I had never thought of the ending quite that way, not until we went to Holcomb, but it read a lot like Capote's: a ripoff, an homage.[98]

For the sake of a book, Capote watched Perry Smith, a man he cared deeply about, swing at the end of a rope; witnesses would later disagree on that point, but I believe he was there, in the room, watching. That moment broke him. He started drinking, really drinking, after Kansas, got deep into pills. Smith's execution would haunt him for the rest of his life; years later, he wrote that if he were drowning, he would see that moment again.[99] Just days after *In Cold Blood*'s release, Capote already seemed to regret writing it. He said that if he'd known what the future held, he would never have stopped in Holcomb: "I would have driven straight on, like a bat out of hell."[100]

I wondered what would've happened if Bonnie and I had never come to Kansas. Some rare moments feel significant even as they happen: the future stretches ahead, flat and forbidding, like a highway across the plains. Capote had one on the courthouse steps, watching Smith get out of a car. Smith had one on the Clutters' lawn before he killed them. I had one leaving Garden City, watching wheat bend in the wind, just like Capote described, and realizing that whatever was happening between Bonnie and me was beyond our

---

98. This is bullshit, by the way. I don't remember stepping on my book.
99. In "Self-Portrait." *Portraits and Observations: The Essays of Truman Capote*, 305.
100. The interview was with the *New York Times*, and is reprinted in an abridged form in Plimpton's oral history. He actually says he would've never stopped in Garden City, but the sentiment applies.

control. That night we made it safely to Salina, where we rented the last hotel room left in town, and fucked like we were about to die, whispering promises. Two years later, we did that drive again, to start a new life in Minnesota. Later, she passed back through Kansas leaving me, and still later I followed, in a breakneck panic, with a ring in my pocket. Capote was right about endings. There are only two kinds, death and the ones we invent.

Bonnie wrote notes for a poem on our trip to Holcomb. They end with a moment that happened a few days after we left Kansas, when we followed my vet-student cousin into a refrigerated basement in St. Paul, where a dead donkey dangled from the ceiling, its eyes and mouth stuffed white with wax. She wrote that I touched her shoulder and she felt a shock and swore she saw the donkey sway. I think she liked the idea of coming full circle, from the slaughterhouse to the meat locker; they even smelled the same. I just liked the sense of peace. The donkey was blind, mute, storyless. Nobody knew who killed it.

PART IV

A Dark Mirror

In Cold Blood was successful in a way no book could be now. Part of that was timing. In 1965, it was still possible for a young writer to make a living off of his writing alone. Magazines were thriving, publishing innovative work by a new generation of American writers, including the forerunners of what would come to be called New Journalism, a genre that helped blaze a trail for Capote's nonfiction novel.[101] Literary books were still part of mainstream American culture: they sold well, were reviewed in newspapers nationwide, and their authors appeared regularly on television. A long-awaited book by a young, controversial writer was a major media

---

101. Capote disavowed the label. In his *NYT* interview with Plimpton, he said New Journalists didn't have "the proper fictional technical equipment," and said "to be a good creative reporter, you have to be a very good fiction writer."

event. If that author was Truman Capote, a self-promotional wizard who'd spent the past few years running around Manhattan telling everyone he'd created a new art form, it was something more than that, a blockbuster in the making. *In Cold Blood* was profiled in *Newsweek* three years before Capote finished it.[102] He sold the movie rights soon after. By the time the book was done, he'd already made millions off of it.

When *In Cold Blood* finally came out, as a four-part series in *The New Yorker* in the fall of '65, issues flew off newstands, broke sales records, and created a sensation Clarke compared to fans of Charles Dickens shouting at arriving British ships, trying to find out if Little Nell was dead.[103] Random House released the book a month later, in the largest first printing the company had ever done. *In Cold Blood* got an eighteen-page spread in *Life*; its title flashed from a billboard over Times Square; Capote's face was on the cover of magazines, all over TV. The book's release was the subject of a short documentary film by the Maysles brothers. The book itself was an instant bestseller—it would go on to become one of the bestselling nonfiction titles of all time—and everyone reviewed it, mostly raves.[104] The

---

102. Clarke, 348.
103. Ibid., 360.
104. Burroughs was a notable exception. In an excoriating personal letter, he told Capote to enjoy his "dirty money," called it a "dull unreadable

New York Times called it one of the greatest promotional successes in publishing history.[105]

It might have been the most successful book release of all time. *In Cold Blood* made its author an international celebrity. In 1966, Truman Capote broke the mold for literary fame: Clarke compares the Capote of that era to a movie idol or a rock star, and says he was the most famous writer in the world. Later that year, Capote threw his legendary Black & White Ball in Manhattan, a star- and royalty-studded affair that was the social event of the decade.

Capote got exactly what he wanted. But writing a tragedy turned his life into one. The book had burned him down. He claimed the ending was so hard to write that it paralyzed his hands, and after its release he complained of constant stress, back pain, terrible dreams. His drinking got worse, the drugs stronger and constant. *In Cold Blood* was a good, long run for Capote, which is more than most writers get, but it ended. He spent the next two decades sinking into addiction and self-caricature.

He remained a celebrity, a constant on TV talk shows, a fixture at the infamous Studio 54; his name never left the papers for long, although he hated the fame, or claimed to. He

---

book," and literally cursed him: "As a writer you are finished." He was at least partly right, but more on that later.

105. William D. Smith, "Advertising: A Success Money Didn't Buy," *New York Times*, December 20, 1966.

became an admitted alcoholic—and, finally, after a handful of failed attempts at rehab, an unapologetic one. He popped a variety of pills, developed a taste for cocaine, had destructive, abusive affairs with married men, one of whom he once hired a hoodlum to assault; he wrecked his car driving drunk, got sued for libel by his old nemesis Gore Vidal, spent a night in a California jail. Perhaps most ominously, Capote began, for the first time in his life, to consistently fail at writing. In 1972, the magazine *Rolling Stone* commissioned him to go on tour with the band of the same name, their first since the nightmare at Altamont three years before,[106] but Capote failed to deliver the article. He spent years working on a documentary film about capital punishment that was never released. For the rest of his life, he claimed to be working on his magnum opus, *Answered Prayers*, what he called "a variation on the nonfiction novel"[107] about elite New York society. A dishy early chapter, "La Côte Basque, 1965," came out in *Esquire*, after which one of the women it was based on committed suicide. The affair made Capote a pariah, and he never finished the book.

Seven years after *In Cold Blood*, Random House,

---

106. The Maysles brothers filmed the Altamont concert for *Gimme Shelter*, capturing the murder of Meredith Hunter, which they then included in the film, another landmark moment in the history of American documentary. We watched it in Charlie's class.
107. In the preface to *Music for Chameleons*, xvi.

perhaps already frustrated by the delay on *Answered Prayers*, put out an anthology of Capote's nonfiction, but most of it was decades old and previously published. Seven years after that, they published another collection of his short pieces, *Music for Chameleons*, a hodgepodge of fiction and nonfiction billed simply as "new writing by Truman Capote." It concludes with a charming, quaaludic interview with himself, in which he discusses his loneliness, addictions, loss of faith; halfway through, he abruptly asks himself about suicide, and mentions that a writer he once knew who later killed himself[108] had said he was certain Capote would, too. But Capote claims he wouldn't have the courage, and mentions that two different fortune tellers had told him he would be lost at sea.

Suicide was often on his mind at the time. While he was writing *Music for Chameleons*, Capote made an infamous appearance on Stanley Siegel's morning TV show in New York. He said he'd come straight from a night of partying, slurred his words, seemed about to fall asleep. When Siegel asked if he'd been drinking, Capote said alcohol was the least of it, "the joker in the deck of cards." Siegel cultivated controversy—he once recreated the execution from Norman Mailer's *The Executioner's Song*, complete

---

108. Yukio Mishima, who committed seppuku in 1970 after a failed attempt to start a coup d'état in Japan.

with on-air gunshots—but even he was shocked by his guest's condition, although not enough to stop the interview. Siegel's subsequent explanation might have made Capote proud: "Someone was telling the truth about themselves on live television," he said. "That's what made it powerful."[109] The clip is still available online, almost fifty years later, both of its principals long since dead. Siegel asks, with what seems to be genuine concern, what's going to happen if his guest keeps going like this. "The obvious answer," Capote says, "is that eventually I'll kill myself, without meaning to."

And so he did, fulfilling all the prophecies, in one way or another: five years later, Capote drowned in a sea of Seconal. His friend Joanne Carson discovered him in her guest room one morning, lying in bed, high as wheat in June, babbling about death. He told her not to call an ambulance.[110] She stayed with him, listening as he spun stories of his youth, his writing, the myth of his forthcoming opus, *Answered Prayers*. Nobody knows if his overdose was intentional or accidental; he made sure the story of his death could not be fully told. When news spread, some of

---

109. This quote is taken from this clip: https://www.youtube.com/watch?v=dh2oWjC-hX0 The phrasing has been changed from the original, but not the content or intent.

110. Officially, he died of complications of liver disease, one of which was multiple drug intoxication. Some have speculated he had AIDS; others that it was suicide. This is more or less Clarke's version, which seems most convincing.

the people who knew him best blamed *In Cold Blood*. They said he was never the same after that.[111]

Music for Chameleons wound up being Capote's last book, or at least the last he lived to see.[112] It sometimes reads like the work of a condemned man. In the title story, a vignette about a visit to Martinique, Capote sits on a terrace with a local aristocrat and discusses food, music, and murder: he mentions that a composer friend of his was killed on the island long ago. The aristocrat sees him looking at a table in the next room, on top of which sits a black mirror, and tries to change the subject. She tells him the mirror once belonged to Paul Gaugin, and that he and other dead artists—Van Gogh, Renoir—used it after working to "refresh their vision." Capote indulges in a long description of the mirror, its silver-blue surface and exact dimensions, the case it rests in. It's more of the same preening, trivial precision he used in all of his nonfiction, constantly reminding the reader that *this is real*. Capote's late work reads like he can't stop repeating himself. Anyway, the mirror: he looks into it and sees himself

---

111. Vidal couldn't resist getting in one last shot: his response was to call Capote's death a good career move.

112. Technically, this isn't true: a short story he wrote about Christmas was published as a standalone book the year before he died. By then, he was no longer writing, and everybody knew he was in trouble, and it seems like his publisher was just getting a head start: once he died, posthumous Capote books—not to mention books about him—would become a cottage industry.

in shades of gray, his face receding "into its endless depths, its corridors of darkness."[113]

The aristocrat changes the subject again, and they make a bet about whether music can lure lizards into the room; she plays a piano, and it does. Capote glances again at the mirror, and sees it mocking him, but he ends with the chameleons assembling to listen, "a Mozartean mosaic."[114] Again, Capote went on too long, seeking a neat, alliterative closure, trying to come full circle. He should have ended with the black mirror.

•

My memoir came out a year after I went to Holcomb. It's hard to discuss your own book; Capote did it all the time, but things have changed since then. More books are published now than ever before,[115] but fewer matter, so writers are supposed to be grateful for any success, however small. My book was a success, in some ways: it got good reviews, made a few year-end lists, won an award. I did readings and panels and university visits, book festivals and conferences, radio interviews, a keynote speech. My book took me across the

---

113. *Music*, 7.
114. Ibid., 12. He really couldn't resist alliterative endings.
115. You can Google this yourself, but for one point of reference, American publishing houses released 30,000 books in 1966, the year *In Cold Blood* was published; in 2013, the year my book came out, they released ten times that many.

country, to places I'd never been; I got to go to Paris twice. It was more than I could have reasonably hoped for, and I was grateful.

But my book didn't sell. As I would later be told, the first week is the only one that matters, and mine sold somewhere in the neighborhood of a thousand copies.[116] That seemed like a lot to me—it was almost the population of my hometown—but didn't to the company that had paid a lot of money to publish it. My publisher called a few weeks later to deliver the bad news that it wasn't selling as well as they'd hoped.[117] My book's epitaph had been written: it was a commercial failure.

I was grateful for the experience. Publishing a book is hard to do, and most writers never get the chance. But not as grateful as I was supposed to be, and not as much as I said I was. I'd spent five years writing the book, and invested too much of my sense of self-worth in it, too much of the meaning I ascribed to my career and life. I'd also spent too much time thinking about *In Cold Blood*; it had seeped into my dreams, and although I knew it was delusional, I wanted my book to have that kind of success, to make me as rich and famous as

---

116. Exact sales numbers are hard to come by, even for the author, and the historical sales data isn't available to me anymore, so this is an estimate based on my memory. It might have been fewer. I doubt it was more.
117. I would later learn from other writers that those calls are a common book-world formality.

Capote had been. Like him, I had a stubborn and arrogant belief in my own talent; it's pretty much a prerequisite for any success in the book world, if you don't come from money.

I had absurd expectations for my book, wanted it to do impossible things. As dumb as it sounds to say it, I thought it would bring my mother back somehow, let me—and the world—remember her as a person, not just another flat and faceless victim. I wanted it to do for domestic violence what *In Cold Blood* did for capital punishment, which was suspended nationwide a year after Capote's book came out. I wanted to counteract another consequence of Capote's book, the flood of tawdry, exploitative murder stories that followed its formula. I wanted to make readers think about what murder stories meant, why they like and consume them, the way they treat victims, what sort of messages they send and reinforce about how violence works in America.

My book accomplished none of that, but it did have other, unforeseen effects. It further damaged my strained relationship with my father, because of how I portrayed him in it, a portrayal I thought was true. It prompted a few dozen people to get in touch with me, often to tell their own stories of losing someone they loved to murder, a phenomenon I had complicated feelings about. It briefly made me a minor authority on murder, an experience I didn't much enjoy. But the most relevant consequence of writing a memoir, one which more or less dictated my current life, was that it got me jobs.

A college professor was another thing I'd sworn never to be. That was after graduate school, not long after Charlie's class. I'd taught for a few years by then, and found it harder than it had looked when I was watching other people do it. I chafed at the hollow authority others invested me with. (In those ways, it was a lot like narrating a nonfiction book.) I decided to do something else, started bartending, applied for other jobs. But the only ones I got were teaching, and I got better at it with practice, and eventually it became the closest thing I had to a career.

Capote often expressed contempt for academics. He didn't go to college, and was made to feel dumb and provincial by the Ivy League crowd in his early years as a writer. But he didn't need the academy; he could pay the bills by writing. He survived his journeyman years by selling work to magazines, and on consistent advances from *The New Yorker* and Random House for things he hadn't written. Those days are dead and buried. I doubt a writer in America makes a living writing short stories anymore, and vanishingly few do it in any genre. Teaching is no longer a fallback option for writers, like it was a generation ago. Full-time jobs have dried up as universities corporatize and exploit contract labor, and the few still left are ruthlessly competitive. I would've never become a professor if I hadn't sold my book. Even then, it took six more years of applications, a dozen surreal interviews in hotel suites, three moves across the country to places I had never been, and who knows how much luck and privilege, before I got a real job.

But I did. Two years after my book came out, and ten since I first read *In Cold Blood*, we moved to Oregon—Bonnie, her son, and I—for my new job as a nonfiction professor at a state university, where I teach Capote's book in my classes. Sometimes it feels like my life is a story he wrote, and I've come full circle, in a way that seems suspiciously neat, and convenient for narrative purposes.

•

In Cold Blood wasn't just an unprecedented success at the time; it has also enjoyed a long, remarkable afterlife as perhaps the most influential work of American nonfiction. The book still sells well, and it entered the canon long ago, as a staple of high school and university classes. The eponymous movie, which Capote consulted on and included scenes shot inside the Clutter house, was released to wide acclaim in 1967. (Ironically, Capote criticized the film for focusing too much on the killers.) Since then, the book has been the subject of two other feature films—including the Academy Award-winning *Capote* in 2005—as well as three plays, two biographies, two fiction novels,[118] another short

---

118. Forgive the use of this barbarism: it seems necessary here, for once, to distinguish from Capote's "nonfiction novel."

documentary, a TV series, an opera, a graphic novel, a book-length critical treatment, dozens of dissertations, hundreds of academic papers and articles, this book, and who knows what else.[119] *In Cold Blood* has stayed relevant for fifty-five years and counting. Since I went to Holcomb in 2012, the two killers have been dug up for DNA tests attempting to link them to another murder, which led to national media attention and a book speculating about their involvement.[120] Harold Nye, one of the KBI detectives featured in *In Cold Blood*, died and left secret case files to his son, who co-wrote a book of his own,[121] and a new documentary TV series about the Clutter murders was recently released.[122] Countless other

---

119. For a full list of artistic works based on *In Cold Blood*, as of 2011, see Voss, 151.

120. The book, JT Hunter's *In Colder Blood*, offers a compelling circumstantial case for Smith and Hickock having killed another family, the Walkers of Osprey, Florida, in strikingly similar circumstances later in 1959. Hunter points out multiple inaccuracies in *In Cold Blood*, which suggests that Smith and Hickock didn't kill the Walkers. Recent DNA tests were inconclusive, but they remain the most likely suspects in the Walker murders, according to local police. If Smith and Hickock did kill the Walkers, that would invalidate Capote's entire theory about the Clutter murders—Smith's "brain explosion"—and make his sympathetic portrayal of them even more problematic. It would also make Capote a pioneer in another sense, the first literary writer to glorify serial killers.

121. *And Every Word Is True* by Gary McIvoy, which was self-published in 2019, presents a possible alternative motive for the Clutter murders, based on Nye's notes and Hickock's correspondence.

122. Sundance TV's *Cold Blooded: The Clutter Family Murders*, directed by Joe Berlinger.

works have been influenced by *In Cold Blood*, whether or not their creators realized it.

Capote did create a new art form, just not the one he thought. It wasn't the "nonfiction novel," which never caught on, and wasn't original, anyway: he likely borrowed that approach from Lillian Ross's *Picture*.[123] Capote wasn't the first writer to make the murderer the protagonist, either: Meyer Levin did that nine years earlier, with *Compulsion*, his novel about the Leopold-Loeb case. But *In Cold Blood* was more successful than its predecessors, and much more influential. Capote spiked a vein, and out came a stream of imitators, a whole bloody genre, one of the most popular forms of American nonfiction: true crime.

In Cold Blood helped launch a national fascination with murder, and especially with murderers themselves. A few years after its release, the Manson family murders riveted the country. In 1974, the prosecutor of the case, Vincent Bugliosi, wrote a nonfiction book of his own, *Helter Skelter*, which would go on to outsell even *In Cold Blood*. Five years later, Norman Mailer won the Pulitzer Prize for his true-crime doorstop, *The Executioner's Song*,[124] a book Capote deeply resented, both for its success—he was still bitter that

---

123. The idea may go back further than that, possibly by centuries—some critics have traced the idea of a nonfiction novel all the way to Daniel Defoe.

124. In fiction, oddly enough.

In Cold Blood hadn't won any national awards—and because he thought his old friend had ripped him off. (He was right in at least one sense: of its thousand-plus pages, Mailer devotes just a few to the victims.) The next year, Ann Rule's *The Stranger Beside Me*, about her friendship with the serial killer Ted Bundy, was a runaway success. In 1986, Robert Graysmith's *Zodiac* followed suit, and on and on.

I came of age in the 1980s, during a true crime boom, surrounded by sensationalized stories about murder. I watched *Unsolved Mysteries* and *America's Most Wanted* on TV, read anthologies with lurid covers in my middle school library, played *Police Quest*—one of the first true-crime video games—on my family's primitive computer. Serial killers were constantly in the news—Gacy, the Nightstalker, Dahmer— and their Hollywood analogs featured in playground conversations, descendants of Norman Bates, many of whom were also based on real murderers: Michael Myers, Jason Voorhees, Pennywise, Hannibal Lecter. In the early 1990s, the O.J. Simpson trial became the first true crime story broadcast live on television. In 1997, Eric Schlosser traced the then-burgeoning national fascination with murderers back to *In Cold Blood*.[125] In 1999, after the Columbine High School shooting, that fascination mutated into a deadly new

---

125. This is also from "A Grief Like No Other." He mentions other origins—Edgar Allen Poe, *Psycho*—but credits Capote with creating a new genre, and helping to take killer-protagonists mainstream.

strain, in which serial killers were largely replaced by mass shooters as emblems of American evil. In 2001, after the nation watched thousands of people die on television in the September 11th attacks, there seemed to be a lull in our true crime fascination, but it's hard for me to say: my mother was murdered eight days later, and for a while after that I wasn't paying attention.[126]

In any case, true crime has recently made a comeback. In 2014, *Serial* came out, and soon became the *In Cold Blood* of podcasts; the story of a cold-case murder in Baltimore, it was the most successful podcast in history, and was soon followed by dozens of imitators; as I write this, six years later, four of the ten most popular podcasts in America are true crime.[127] Meanwhile, TV shows like *The Jinx* and *Making a Murderer* became the streaming equivalents, episodic true-crime stories that captivated huge audiences. CrimeCon, an annual true crime convention, launched in 2017; multiple cities have true crime walking tours or live-action role playing games; there's even a monthly subscription box called Hunt a Killer. True crime has become our national obsession.

•

126. There may not have been a lull at all, or not a long one, at least: Voss mentions a 2009 *Newsweek* cover article titled "True Crime: An American Obsession," 97.
127. According to Apple's podcast rankings.

I can't stand true crime. I certainly don't write it. These days, I mostly write this kind of thing, which fits somewhere within the woefully named category of creative nonfiction. The term didn't exist when Capote was alive, and I wonder what he'd think of the genre it denotes. On one hand, it's more or less the new art form he helped invent; on the other, nobody uses his term for it, and creative nonfiction is practiced mostly in dusty corners of academia. Creative nonfiction writers talk adoringly about Montaigne, name textbooks after Emily Dickinson quotations, and endlessly cite the origins of the term "essay," which—as you already know, if you've read any essays lately—comes from old French, *essai*, to attempt.[128] I stumbled into the cloisters of creative nonfiction after fleeing the dreary, tapestried halls of contemporary fiction.

Today, the essay is all the rage; it's the contemporary version of Capote's nonfiction novel, a new form of nonfiction that's going to revolutionize the form. A subgenre of creative nonfiction, the essay is an act of sensemaking: it separates, arranges, and presents factual material as what it really is, data that requires interpretation. Creative nonfiction people say the essay is a natural progression away from narrative, toward inquiry: curation of data, an acknowledgment of

---

128. Like the thing it describes, that's only true in the loosest sense of the word—see John Jeremiah Sullivan's introduction to the 2014 edition of *Best American Essays*.

multiple interpretations. They say it's the form of the future. But it seems like everyone who says that is a teacher or student in an MFA program, and although I've learned to love essays, as far as I can tell, only a few thousand people in America care much about them. So it should be no surprise that essay classes are a tough sell to undergraduates, who don't know what the term means—they usually associate it with the five-paragraph kind their high school teachers made them write—and, in my experience, are not especially interested in spending ten weeks finding out. After several consecutive quarters of low enrollments, I tried to come up with nonfiction courses that might fill more seats. So I made a deal with the devil: I started teaching true crime.

True Crime 101[129] focuses on American true crime works, for reasons both practical—we only have ten weeks, I don't know British literature nearly as well—and philosophical: one of the implicit arguments is that true crime is an American creation, a black mirror reflecting our collective fears and preoccupations. That's what the syllabus says, at least: as I write this, I am teaching the course for the first time, so I'm flying by the seat of my pants.

We start three centuries before Capote, with a paragraph from William Bradford's history of Plymouth about the

---

129. This is not the actual name or course number, but it is what I usually call it. I'm also fictionalizing all the students and their comments, to protect their anonymity.

colony's first execution. In 1630, a Pilgrim named John Billington shot and killed another man during a quarrel. The colonists tried Billington and hung him in public. This wasn't the first true story about a crime. Indigenous oral traditions tell of crimes and their effects on a community, and the Bible was the prototype for colonial crime stories. Bradford's isn't even the first written account of a murder in what is now America: Spanish writers had been publishing chronicles of torture, murder, and genocide in the Caribbean for a century before him. But the story of John Billington is one of the first examples written in English in what is now America. Besides, it's in the textbook.[130]

On the first day of class, by the time we read about John Billington, I've introduced myself, made a few tense attempts at humor, gone over the syllabus, and answered a few questions that are mostly about whether I take attendance. Just as my students are starting to whisper, rustle papers, dig in bags, performing their desire to leave, I put the text up on the projector, read the paragraph out loud, and ask what they notice. I don't expect much, but they're game: we list on the board a few characteristics of Bradford's account that might apply to other true crime. Some are examples of what I call, for purposes of the class,

---

130. Harold Schecter's *True Crime: An American Anthology*. Library of America, 2008.

truth claims, or ways a text asserts its basis in reality: real places, real people, real names, and so on. We discuss how the term "true crime" is itself a truth claim, implying that crime is somehow fictional. We talk about what kind of crimes the genre covers—murder, mostly—and what aspects of those crimes it focuses on. Bradford is a useful example. Three hundred years before true crime existed, he seems to inherently understand something about how an American murder story should be told, not just the crime itself, but the investigation, the trial, the execution, the effect on the community. We might as well be talking about Capote, but that'll be another few weeks.

I had planned to spend the first month or so of the class working our way through the early years of the genre, with precursors of modern true crime. There's a lot of good stuff in the textbook: Cotton Mather, Ben Franklin, Hawthorne, Twain, Mitchell, Mencken, Liebling. But before our first class ends, a student informs me that the campus bookstore doesn't have our textbook in stock. After class, I call the bookstore, and the plot thickens. The employee suggests I may have forgotten to order it. I tell him I have evidence that proves otherwise. He says there might be a problem on the publisher's end. At the beginning of our next class, I suggest we launch an investigation, break into groups and delegate tasks: call the publisher, find the invoice, maybe even do a FOIA request for the bookstore's emails—it's a state university, so they're public records—talk to the principals involved, visit the warehouse, crack the case of the missing textbooks, solve our own true crime. My students endure my lame attempt at humor for a few minutes, then mercifully interrupt and ask what we're going to do. I shrug and tell them we'll just spend more time on *In Cold Blood*. It's easier for me, anyway: I can teach that book in my sleep.

The upshot of the textbook snafu is that I only get to teach two more texts from the long tradition of true crime before Capote. One is a brief article from 1846 about a bizarre murder case in Illinois, written by Abraham Lincoln, then a young lawyer whose prose shows glimpses of the president he would become: halting eloquence, a humble concision. Lincoln tells the story of a murder without a body; I won't ruin the rest. In class, we compare Lincoln to Bradford. Both take the same general approach, a detached observer relating the facts of a murder. Both authors appear only once, near the end, as hesitant narrators confessing gaps in their knowledge. Lincoln's article is much longer and more detailed than Bradford's, and goes deeper into the investigation, not only the crime and punishment. It gives a clearer sense of a story being told, one with an Aristotalean dramatic structure: beginning, middle, end. Bradford lapses into first person once, to admit that he doesn't know a minor part of the story, but Lincoln refuses to put himself in the text, instead adding an entire closing paragraph in third person, speculating on what might have happened. *Just like Capote*, I think, but I don't say it in class. They'll see for themselves.

The last thing we read before *In Cold Blood* is Zora Neale Hurston's "The Trial of Ruby McCollum," written seven years before Capote went to Kansas. Hurston's essay, about the case of a black woman accused of killing a white doctor in Florida, shows just how full of shit Capote was to claim he invented a new genre. Hurston was another esteemed Alabama author, and, like Capote, she'd published a handful of successful books, both fiction and nonfiction, before she turned to writing crime. But Hurston showing up in a small Southern town to ask questions about a local murder was a very different proposition from even Capote's cold reception in Holcomb. Then as now, crime writers were predominantly white and male, facts that suggest a story of their own, one about power and authority, whose stories get told and who gets to tell them. The sheriff refused to allow Hurston (or "outsiders," as he put it) to talk to the accused, and the courthouse was segregated, so she had to watch the trial from the balcony. But Hurston also had access no white writer would've: she could walk into a local black cafe and talk freely with its patrons about the case. Like Bradford and Lincoln before her, Hurston focuses on the impact the crime has on the community; unlike them, she acknowledges more than one community.

Hurston also puts herself on the page, in first person,

and makes no claim to objectivity. In fact, subjectivity is the point: Hurston's story is a black perspective on the case, a sort of counterweight to the dominant narrative being told in the white-owned media. Her narrator is less concerned with facts, and seems to inherently understand the way they can be framed to reflect the desires of power, made into a simple story to be spoken in its halls. Hurston has an agenda; she's a witness, an advocate, and she doesn't pretend otherwise. Unlike Capote.

•

I teach *In Cold Blood* now, so I read it a lot, and know it better than any other book, possibly including my own. But my favorite of Capote's books is *Music for Chameleons*. I didn't get around to reading it until recently, and it's a strange little volume, made up of thirteen short pieces, a mixture of fiction and nonfiction, the last things he ever wrote.

The preface is a memoirish account of his writerly life. He describes his career in three cycles. The first is his apprenticeship and early publications, up to his first book. The second cycle covers the next ten years, a productive decade during which he experiments with different forms and techniques, writing and publishing in multiple genres and realms. He wrote short stories, movie scripts, plays, and nonfiction—what he calls "essays and portraits"—as well as *The Muses Are Heard*, a novella-length work of reportage which he describes as a prototype for the nonfiction novel. In Capote's telling, his second cycle was an ascent to mastery, and ended with the short novel *Breakfast at Tiffany's*, published when he was thirty-four. The third cycle was *In Cold Blood*, an era unto itself. He describes the fourth cycle as his last, and says it began once he'd been ostracized from Manhattan's high society for his caustic portrayals of its denizens. He found himself in a creative crisis, one that changed his "understanding of the difference between what is true and what is *really* true."[131]

Capote reveals that he reread *In Cold Blood* and discovered that it wasn't as good as it could've been. In fact, he read everything he'd ever written, and the feeling was universal: he realized he had never been working with more than half of his powers. So he asked himself a simple question—why?—which led to a much more complicated one, the heart of the matter. He'd spent all those years writing in different forms, learning and mastering the techniques of screenwriting, drama, fiction, and nonfiction. But he'd been restricting himself within those forms, not applying the techniques across genres—in other words, not synthesizing his talents, bringing them all to bear at once. The crisis led

---

131. *Music for Chameleons*, xvii. All quotes in this passage are from pages xvii–xviii.

him to a question: "How can a writer successfully combine within a single form . . . all he knows about every other form of writing?"

So Capote experimented, and found an answer. Until then, he had tried to make himself "as invisible as possible" in his reportage; he says the greatest difficulty of *In Cold Blood* was leaving himself out of the book completely. So he tried the opposite, putting himself "center stage" as he interviewed everyday people. Over time, he says, he developed a new style, and *Music for Chameleons* is the result. Capote doesn't name his new style; maybe he learned something from the failure of his term "nonfiction novel." But what he's talking about, a form that blends the techniques of multiple genres, using a distinct and deeply subjective perspective to describe real events, has a name. It's called an essay. Once Capote got sick of true crime, it was all he wanted to write. Turns out we had more in common than I knew.

•

Before we start discussing *In Cold Blood*, I give the class some context. First, the backstory; Capote's old chestnut about finding the newspaper article and having a revelation. After that, I tell them the real story, how Capote went to Kansas write an article, that Harper Lee went with him, and so on. I ask if anybody has read *In Cold Blood* before. Nobody has, but they all know *To Kill a Mockingbird*, so I tell them Dill was based on Capote, and talk a bit about his early career, fame, and personality. I show a brief clip of him being interviewed, so they can hear his infamous voice, see his charm at work, and understand how he might have had a hard time in Holcomb, at least at first.

The clip is from the Maysles brothers documentary *A Visit With Truman Capote*,[132] released early in 1966, as *In Cold Blood* was taking over the world. In class, I only show the first few minutes, to give a sense of the man behind the book, before we move on to the opening pages, how Capote sets the stage: his focus on community and tragedy, the silos rising like Greek temples and the townspeople as a chorus and so on; the alternating portrayals of the Clutters and their killers, the book's starkly different sympathies.

I try to avoid the topic of truth, at least at first, but my students aren't the readers of Capote's era. Like all generations' theories about the next, mine are anecdotal, skewed by nostalgia, and punitive, projections of my own atavistic fears of death and irrelevance. But in the last few years, as my classes have transitioned from late millennials, more or less my own

132. It's also apparently known as *With Love From Truman*. The opening credits make the title unclear: they show Capote's inscription on a copy of *In Cold Blood*, a handwritten "With Love From Truman," above two other superimposed subtitles: *The Nonfiction Novel* and *A Visit With Truman Capote*.

generation, to a distinct new generation—postmillennials, Gen Z, whatever—I've noticed a shift in my students' attitudes about truth. It's not just them: American ideas of truth have changed since Capote went to Kansas. He began *In Cold Blood* during the Eisenhower era of prosperous postwar conservatism, an environment his portrayal of the Clutters was probably meant to critique. But in the years Capote spent writing the book, he saw his friend John F. Kennedy elected president, ushering in a new and turbulent era of lies and conspiracies: the Bay of Pigs, JFK's assassination, the country blundering deeper into war in Vietnam. By the time *In Cold Blood* was released, the sixties were roiling America's belief system, and the idea of a shared and definite truth has taken a beating ever since. The generation before mine remembers My Lai, Watergate; we had Iran-Contra, the Clinton impeachment, 9/11. My current students were born during our endless, factless war in Iraq, and grew up with social media, the death blow for any notion of collective truth, and smartphones, the black mirrors of the present.[133] They've been bombarded by spun facts, equivocations, and outright lies for their entire lives. My class takes place in 2020, four years into the Trump administration, a moment when truth itself is a partisan issue, and arguably less relevant than ever before. I've

---

133. The tech-anxiety horror show *Black Mirror* took its name from how a smartphone screen looks when turned off.

spent the last few years standing in front of rooms of young adults, discussing the concept of truth; they don't seem to care all that much about it, or believe that it exists, and it's hard to blame them. We don't even talk much about truth in class: we talk about truth *claims*, the ways a text convinces you to believe it. On the first day of discussing *In Cold Blood*, when I tell the class Capote claimed every word of it was true, somebody asks what that even *means*.

I don't know the answer, but if we had time, I'd show the rest of *A Visit With Truman Capote* as a way of trying to find one. The documentary is a case study in true portrayals, a hall of mirrors: the best-known film documentarians of their era, making a movie about its best-known nonfiction writer, as he's interviewed by a prominent reporter for a major national magazine, everybody creating their own version of the truth. The film follows Capote around for a day promoting his book, then to his cottage in the Hamptons, while his interviewer, Karen Gundersen of *Newsweek*, asks questions about his new book, and he gives answers that already seem practiced.

The presence of the Maysles brothers was another in a long and remarkable line of coincidences that helped make *In Cold Blood* arguably the most influential work of American nonfiction in any medium. The Maysles and their editor, Charlotte Zwerin, were rising stars themselves, part of the Direct Cinema movement then doing for documentary film what Capote did for nonfiction writing, pioneering a new kind of true story. The coincidences didn't stop there: the Maysles' had, like Capote, first tested their new approach in Russia, and were looking for a subject for the major new work that would define their approach. Truman Capote's new book wasn't it: the short documentary would soon fade into obscurity, before YouTube eventually revived it. But during the filming of *A Visit With Truman*, Capote's editor, Joe Fox, suggested the Maysles make a film about traveling salesmen. They did, and three years later released *Salesman*, the movie that made them documentary icons and changed the form forever.[134]

What interests me most about *A Visit With Truman* is that it shows what happens when more than one artist is present. Between Capote, the Maysles, and Karen Gundersen—one of the pioneering female journalists of the era, who interviews Capote in the film—three nonfiction experts collide, each with different agendas, each exerting their own calculated controls on the stories being told. Capote is outnumbered, and the balance of power shifts: he becomes the subject. He seems uncomfortable at the prospect. Although widely known as a character, Capote was never much of an actor. His late-in-life acting debut, in the 1976 Neil Simon comedy *Murder by Death*, met with

---

134. For more on *Salesman*, its similarities to *In Cold Blood*, direct cinema, the Maysles, objectivity, and so forth, consult J.M. Tyree's excellent book, *Salesman* (BFI Film Classics, 2012.).

withering reviews, even though the character was created for and based on him; as his biographer put it, "he did not play a convincing Truman Capote."[135]

The documentary was filmed just days after *In Cold Blood* came out, but you can already see how nervous and self-conscious fame has made him, how he's begun to play the part of himself. Capote quotes an early rejection from *The New Yorker* verbatim, revealing his famed ability to hold grudges. He almost sheepishly shows the camera pictures from Kansas, handling the ones of Perry Smith with an exaggerated reverence. At one point, while reading the book's first description of Smith aloud, Capote makes a prim, calculating revision: instead of reading the actual text, in which Dick tells Perry he stares in the mirror like he was looking at "some gorgeous piece of butt," Capote changes it to "some gorgeous girl," eliding one of the book's few clanging lines, and deftly concealing its homosexual subtext, as he would in the months to come.

Soon Gundersen dispenses with the preliminaries and starts asking questions. At first, Capote's answers are the same schtick he'd practiced for years at parties: *In Cold Blood* is "a completely factual account"; his original interest in the book was the "aesthetic theory" of mixing journalism

135. Clarke, *Capote*, 475. Clarke blames Capote's overacting on his lifelong anxiety, which worsened after *In Cold Blood*, as he aged and tried different ways to medicate it.

and fictional technique; he wrote it not for personal gain, but to force recognition of his new art form; and so on. But Gundersen was nobody's fool: she'd interviewed bigger and more dangerous bullshitters than Capote.[136] She asks Capote a probing question about his relationship with the killers, which seems to catch him off guard. He removes his glasses, rubs his furrowed brow, and calls Perry Smith "a strange and difficult boy." His answer wanders and halts as he admits to getting closer to Perry than he did to Dick, calling his relationship with the former "a very intimate, very intense sort of friendship," before walking that back: "I don't know if friendship is exactly the word, but some kind of very intense relationship having to do with his total loneliness, and my feelings of pity for him, and even a kind of affection." Quickly, though, Capote recovers his typical poise. When Gundersen asks a challenging question about where he got the information to write a specific scene in such detail, he gives a longwinded answer about the five years he spent with the killers, interviewing them over and over until he got everything he needed.

Later in the film, Capote discusses his friendship with the Deweys, and mentions that they had come to visit him in New York a few weeks earlier. The filmmakers do a subtle, perhaps seminal jump-cut to footage of that visit, a shot

---

136. Henry Kissinger, for one example.

of Alvin Dewey standing on the ice at Rockefeller Center. Capote continues as a voiceover, a narrator interpreting the action onscreen as he takes them to see the sights. They go to Random House, where he shows the Deweys promotional materials for the book. They wander New York, walking by Tiffany's, cracking breakfast jokes. At a window with a view of the city, in what might have been Capote's then-new apartment at UN Plaza, Marie Dewey asks him to point out the Statue of Liberty; Capote laughs at the suggestion, then takes them on a ferry ride to see it.

It's the closest thing I've ever seen to a real portrayal of Truman Capote, his boyish laugh and alacritous wit, the warm, wounded narcissism that he made seem so charming. At the end of the ferry ride, after a close shot of Alvin Dewey's stoic, misplaced face, the film makes another jump cut, back to Capote's house in the Hamptons, where the camera zooms in on a photo of Perry Smith, handcuffed and flanked by police, perhaps walking to the gallows. Capote talks about the death row years, his visits to the Corner, and shows Gundersen a box of letters the killers sent him, twice a week, for five years. He reads snippets of two out loud, chuckling at Perry's self-important prose. But soon he has to stop. "Oh," he says, "I shouldn't have opened up this." The camera zooms in on the author as his mouth tries to decide what to do. He says he hasn't looked at the letters in so long; it was a sad thing to do. "God, god, god, god," he whispers. "Save us all."

Capote is lying on a chaise longue by this point, rubbing his shut eyes and sniffling. He tells the story of the execution, insisting he was there,[137] explaining why he narrated it in Dewey's point of view. He reads his made-up ending as the film cuts again, to a panning shot of Valley View; it stops and zooms in on the Clutter grave. "The end," Capote says, and stares directly into the camera. In that moment, before he has to look away, you can see, written on his face, what the book had done to him. He says he knew it had to end on that scene, "moving you back into real, ordinary life." But that scene was fake, and there was no ordinary life for him to return to, not after *In Cold Blood*. The film ends with a clip of he and Gundersen walking on an empty, windswept beach. Capote removes his hat and makes a joke about the wind blowing through his thinning hair. "The aging poet," he says, and laughs. The end.

•

The centerpiece of *Music for Chameleons* is "Hardcarved Coffins: A Nonfiction Account of an American Crime," a novella-length work that reads like a half-hearted sequel to *In Cold Blood*. Both pieces open in exactly the same way, with the description of a small Western town wracked by

---

137. This clip is why I believe him.

murders, the same distant, detached perspective. Quickly, however, we see that things are going to different. For one thing, Capote is in the novella, and not only as an omniscient third-person narrator, like he was in *In Cold Blood*, deciding what went where. This time he's writing in the first person, acting as both a character and the narrator. He's not even pretending to be objective; he's putting himself on the page, his words and thoughts, talents and sensibilities, his writerly mind. He's implicated, responsible, possibly even in danger himself.

Of course, none of it's true. If Capote described his approach to *In Cold Blood* as planting a seed in the reader's mind and letting the story grow, "Handcarved Coffins" reads more like he doodled a tree on a piece of paper, pointed to it, and told the reader it was real. A ludicrous, campy murder mystery right out of Agatha Christie, it's hard to imagine anyone, Capote included, ever believing it was true.[138]

It's tempting to read "Handcarved Coffins" as a sort of self-satire, Capote cynically cashing in on the true crime boom he helped create by giving readers what they seemed to want. In the years since *In Cold Blood*, the genre had exploded, thanks to Bugliosi and Mailer, and a few weeks after *Music for Chameleons* came out, Rule's *The Stranger Beside Me* became the next in a long line of massively popular murder books. In

---

138. Christie was one of Capote's favorite writers.

her history of American true crime,[139] Jean Murley explains the true-crime conventions of the era: a lack of ambiguity, the rhetoric of good vs. evil, as much gore as possible, and a focus on the killer that had only grown stronger since *In Cold Blood*. If that's what readers wanted, Capote seems to have decided, that's what he'd give them.

In "Handcarved Coffins," Capote drops the reins on his Gothic tendencies and cranks up the bullshit. A serial killer in the obscure West—the town and state are never named—has been mailing tiny wooden coffins as warnings before murdering his victims in exotic ways: drug-injected rattlesnakes, burning them alive, beheading. Enter Jake Pepper, the detective in charge of the case, a raffish literary descendant of Alvin Dewey, whom Capote claims introduced them. Behind it all, a murky water dispute, a town living in fear. When the detective's paramour receives a coffin of her own, a showdown at the suspect's ranch ensues. It's a fun read, tense and entertaining; Capote could really tell a story. But the best part is that he said it was all true, and, once again, a lot of people believed him.

When he wrote "Handcarved Coffins," Capote was desperate. He hadn't produced a book in several years, and had missed deadline after deadline for *Answered Prayers*.

---

139. *The Rise of True Crime: 20th Century Murder and American Popular Culture*, Praeger, 2008. This is the best history of true crime I've read.

Most of his friends had disowned him after the scandal over "La Côte Basque, 1965," and Random House had all but given up on him. So Capote combined elements of different cases Dewey had told him about, and—without asking for his friend's permission—cranked out a Gothic novella he decided to call nonfiction. Dewey was outraged: he'd planned to write a book of his own, and felt like Capote had ripped him off.[140]

A decade later, a pair of British reporters named Peter and Leni Gillman picked "Handcarved Coffins" apart. They discovered that it was based primarily on a case Dewey investigated, a 1974 double murder in Ensign, Kansas, an hour's drive from Holcomb. But the Ensign case had only a passing resemblance to Capote's version: it "had merely served as the starting point for a blend of fact and fiction, reportage and fantasy."[141] The Gillmans called it "one of the great literary hoaxes."

Music for Chameleons got mixed reviews, more in line with the tepid critical reception of Capote's early work than the effusive praise for *In Cold Blood*. But many critics raved

---

140. All of this information is from Gillman, Peter & Leni, "Hoax: Secrets that Truman Capote Took to the Grave," (London) *Sunday Times Magazine*, June 21, 1992. Accessed here: http://reprints.longform.org/hoax-truman-capote-secret. I heartily recommend reading the whole article. Among other trenchant observations, they suggest that one character in "Handcarved Coffins" may be based on Herb Clutter.
141. Ibid.

about "Handcarved Coffins," comparing it favorably to its ancestor, and *Music* became a bestseller. Capote soon sold the movie rights to "Handcarved Coffins" for three hundred grand. Whenever anybody—his editor at Random House, the producer who bought the rights—pressed Capote for details on the true story behind the novella, he claimed he couldn't share it, for legal reasons. "Handcarved Coffins" was the last substantial thing Capote wrote. He continued to claim it was true, "exactly what happened,"[142] until the day he died.

•

In True Crime 101, we break *In Cold Blood* into chunks: seventy pages for each Tuesday class, thirty more by Thursday. Along the way, I share some supplementary materials, articles about the book, clips of Capote on television shows talking about his methods. The class is new to me, so I approach it like I would writing an essay, with only a vague sense of what it is, a handful of key concepts to cover. We'll discuss the book's illusion of objectivity, its heavy identification with the killer, the way Capote grafts a tragic arc onto a fact-based story, and his use of techniques that blur the line between fact and fiction: dramatizations, reconstructions, scenes invented out of whole cloth. The usual suspects.

---

142. Ibid.

Most days, I open class by asking my students what they noticed, what stuck out, what seemed interesting. That way they're marginally more engaged, and I get to hear what it's like to read *In Cold Blood* for the first time. True Crime 101 fulfills a core requirement for graduation, so the class is not the bunch of bookish sophisticates that might populate an upper-division lit course. This group is twenty-seven undergraduates culled mostly from the greater Willamette Valley, diverse in year, major, identity, and academic background. Their only commonalities are place and choice of college and, judging by their decision to enroll in the class, at least a passing interest in true crime—except for the few who have already, unwisely, told me they only took the class because it starts at noon. True Crime 101 is the closest thing I'm going to see to a cross-section of the contemporary American reading public.

I figured we would start by discussing truth. It's a natural departure point, a concept we already have a framework for, questions we can ask: is *In Cold Blood* true? How do we know? And we do, for the first few minutes of our first class about Capote. We talk about dialogue, detail, access: how he didn't use a tape recorder, or even a notebook, preferring to go back to the hotel afterward and type interviews from memory. A student raises her hand, says she's done a lot of interviewing, and thinks that's impossible: memory isn't that accurate. I say that's a good point—and it is, although I always say that[143]—and show a clip of Capote explaining his methods of transcription. It's from a TV interview in 1967,[144] just before the movie adaptation of *In Cold Blood* came out. When asked how he recorded the book's extensive dialogue, Capote claims to have "the auditory version of a photographic memory." He says it comes naturally, but he also practiced for two years; he describes a convoluted process involving tape recorders. He doesn't say it in this clip, but sometimes Capote claimed to have tested his memory for accuracy. The trouble was, the number kept changing from one interview to the next, from 94 to 95 to 96 percent recall. As George Plimpton put it, "He could recall everything, but he could never remember what percentage recall he had."[145]

As the class gets deeper into the book, we track the obvious developments: Perry Smith's emergence as the most sympathetic character, Capote's use of dramatic irony to drive the plot. My students seem to see it, and not just in the sense that they nod and agree: they notice things I

---

143. My students know this; they sometimes make fun of me for it.

144. The YouTube description misdates the interview as happening in 1968, but Capote mentions that the movie version of *In Cold Blood* is forthcoming, and it was released in December of 1967. The clip seems to be from *Good Company*, a series hosted by the celebrity lawyer F. Lee Bailey in which he interviewed celebrities in their homes. (The clip is shot at Capote's house in the Hamptons.) https://www.youtube.com/watch?v=TiSiNgaQBYE

145. "Some Thoughts on Capote," *New York Times*, August 26, 1984.

never have, like the frequent parentheticals, especially in Smith's sections, another way to get deeper into his head. The question of truth persists, but begins to take a back seat to bigger ones: what the book's about, what Capote's trying to say.

When we discuss the fourth and final section of *In Cold Blood*, I read out loud the moment on the courthouse steps, Capote's first encounter with the killers. I read them Harper Lee's quote about a great love affair. We discuss how the book shifts away from story, now that all the questions have been answered, the dramatic irony and tension dispelled. It becomes an argument. *If you want to know what a text is about*, I say, *figure out what words it says the most*. I try not to linger in the self-analysis that follows, where I wonder if that statement is true, whether I actually believe it or am saying it for the sake of utility, trying to spin the study of literature into some more practical application that might justify my continued employment in an increasingly capitalist version of academia—and America—that sees books only as products.[146] When this happens, more and more these days, the best thing to do is shut up, so I ask what is probably a stupid question: What words does Capote say the most?

---

146. As far as I can tell, the word that appears most often in this book (articles and conjunctions excluded) is "Capote," with more than 400 mentions. I don't think it's about him.

I wait out the silence, scanning faces. "Anybody?"

"Capital punishment," says a young woman near the back of the room. So far, my experience teaching true crime agrees with the research: despite its gory sensationalism, its hardboiled bluster, and its history as a genre defined mostly by men, other genders seem to like and understand it best.

We go on to briefly discuss Capote's treatment of the execution itself, and how he added Perry Smith's apology in one last bid to sway the reader. How some witnesses said Capote had to leave the warehouse because he couldn't stand to watch. I'm trying not to talk as much this quarter,[147] so I show them another video clip, from a Kansas nightly news program on the fiftieth anniversary of the execution of Smith and Hickock.[148] The 2015 segment includes archival footage from 1965: a brief clip of Hickock being walked down a hall in chains, shots of the prison itself—it's suitably Gothic, one thing Capote didn't have to embellish—and a description of the execution by the reporter, Art Wilson, one of the media witnesses who watched alongside Capote. Wilson looks drawn and speaks haltingly, obviously shaken by the experience, a feeling he calls remorse: "by being a part of this society, I played a part in this execution." He mentions the

---

147. This is my goal pretty much every quarter, which itself suggests some things.

148. The network is KAKE, an ABC affiliate out of Wichita. https://www.youtube.com/watch?v=ZhmlEkDezAY.

twenty-two minutes Hickock dangled from the rope before he was pronounced dead,[149] before ending with a plea that seems to echo the book's: "What I saw tonight," Miller says, "I saw no purpose."

Capote probably never saw the clip, or I'm guessing he would've included it in the book. *In Cold Blood*'s closing pages are one long argument against capital punishment. Capote creates the effect mostly through selection. The characters who oppose the death penalty—the defense attorneys, Bonnie Clutter's brother, the killers and their families—are given the space to say why. The ones who support Smith and Hickock's executions, presumably most of the town, generally don't. Whatever you think about the issue, it's hard to argue that Capote made *In Cold Blood* into much more than a good story, and its commercial success was only part of the reason for its enduring legacy. Not long after Smith and Hickock were executed, George York and James Latham, a pair of spree killers who make a cameo near the end of the book, made their own walk to the warehouse. They were the last people executed by the state of Kansas, as of this writing, and among the last ever killed by hanging in the United States. The year after *In Cold Blood*'s release, America began a

---

149. Wilson doesn't say which killer in the clip, but Capote describes Hickock hanging for twenty minutes. He doesn't describe Smith's hanging much at all—Dewey closes his eyes and hears the sound—which may support the theory that he left the warehouse beforehand.

nationwide hiatus from executions that would last a decade, and in 1972, the Supreme Court ruled capital punishment unconstitutional, and commuted all existing death penalty convictions to life in prison.[150] It's hard to say how much of that was a result of *In Cold Blood*, but whatever else we can say about Capote's choices—all the lies he told, how much he loved the murderer—his book probably saved lives. The lives of murderers, not victims, but lives, all the same. How many books can say that?

•

One of the spared was Bobby Beausoleil, a member of the Manson family. Beausoleil committed the family's first murder, torturing his friend Gary Hinman for days before stabbing him, smothering him with a pillow, using his blood to write messages on the walls of his house, and stealing his car. *Music for Chameleons* includes an interview Capote did with Beausoleil in San Quentin shortly after the Supreme Court ruling that saved him from the gas chamber.

In Cold Blood was not Capote's last polemic against capital punishment, nor was it the last time he would make the acquaintance of murderers. His experience working with

---

150. Four years later, the death penalty was effectively reinstated by *Gregg v. Georgia*.

the Maysles brothers on *A Visit With Truman Capote* made him interested in other forms of nonfiction storytelling; once he was done consulting on the movie version of *In Cold Blood*, he began working on a documentary film, *Death Row, USA*, which he convinced ABC to commission. He finished the film in 1968, but the network refused to air it, calling it "too grim"; Capote responded, "What were you expecting—*Rebecca of Sunnybrook Farm*?"[151] He would later write that *Death Row, USA* was never shown in this country, "for reasons still mysterious and unexplained,"[152] although that seems to have been a lie: a *Time* article from later that year claims Capote bought the rights from ABC and held a private screening for critics in Manhattan, who thought it "lacked organization and a coherent point of view."[153] Four years later, ABC aired a late-night special called *Truman Capote Behind Prison Walls*, which included an interview with Beausoleil, and received similarly dismal reviews.[154]

---

151. Clarke, 413.

152. In the essay "Self-Portrait." See *Portraits and Observations: The Essays of Truman Capote*, 301.

153. "Truman and TV," 11/28/1968. An article with the same title as the film was published in *Esquire*. The film itself included an interview with Ronald Reagan, then the governor of California, which began an unlikely friendship between the Reagans and Capote. (Or so I've read—I haven't been able to see the film.)

154. *Behind Prison Walls* must have been either an updated version of *Death Row, U.S.A.*, or a different film entirely: it includes his interview with Beausoleil, which occurred four years after the latter film was

Capote's interview with Beausoleil[155] later appeared as an essay, "Then It All Came Down." Capote opens by telling his interlocutor that he's just spoken to Sirhan Sirhan; he mentions that he also knew Sirhan's victim, Robert Kennedy, and that he'd known both Kennedy's brother and his assassin, Lee Harvey Oswald, as well as four of the five people Beausoleil's friends killed at Sharon Tate's house in a failed attempt to exonerate him.[156] "I'd say you're not such a lucky guy to know," Beausoleil says. They discuss the gas chamber, and Capote mentions having seen Smith and Hickock hang; he claims he vomited afterwards. Capote comments on his subject's tattoos; Beausoleil strums a guitar; the author notices how his face changes at different angle; they discuss his dreams of having a musical career one day.[157] Capote might as well be writing about Perry Smith. But Beausoleil

---

finished. The *San Francisco Bay Guardian* called the former "desperately commercial" and "lip-smackingly voyeuristic." ("Prison Verite," by Larry Peitzman, Jan. 17, 1973.) The *New York Times* was no kinder: "After an hour and a half, it prompts a single question: Why?" ("TV: A Diverse Trio—Ireland, Jail and Rothschilds," by John J. O'Connor, Dec. 7, 1972.)

155. The essay mentions Beausoleil being thirty-one at the time, which would place it in 1978, six years after the documentary. But the dialogue seems to suggest it was their first meeting, in 1972.

156. The coincidences don't end there: Plimpton, one of Capote's eventual biographers, was standing near RFK when he was shot, and was one of the people who subdued Sirhan.

157. Beausoleil was an early member of the eminent LA rock band Love, and has released a number of albums from prison, including the score for the Kenneth Anger film *Lucifer Rising*.

is still alive, so he still has agency: he would later publicly object to the portrayal, and claim that Capote fictionalized the interview.[158]

Capote published "Then It All Came Down" in a section of *Music for Chameleons* called "Conversational Portraits." He wrote most of the pieces in the book during his last period of productivity, for Andy Warhol's magazine, *Interview*. Capote probably thought of them as articles; fiction writers still do this sort of thing, writing nonfiction as promotion for their "real" books, articles they insist on calling essays. But Capote's *were* essays. That's how I think of them, at least: gleefully unconcerned with objectivity or factual truth, freed from the artificial architecture of story, short and weird and voicy, so much fun to read, a window into his mind. In one of them, he follows a cleaning lady through her workday, which ends with them getting stoned, raiding a client's fridge, eating all of the ice cream, getting caught, and quitting. In other pieces in *Music*, Capote confesses his alcoholism, drug addiction, sexual and suicidal fantasies; refers to himself as a genius; discusses his brief acquaintance with Willa Cather; calls Robert Frost an "evil, selfish bastard"; claims to have slept with Errol Flynn; and narrates a day spent dodging police trying to arrest him on a warrant. His essay on Marilyn

---

158. See Beausoleil's Facebook page: https://m.facebook.com/notes/bobby-beausoleil/the-capote-interview/992784917403821.

Monroe is the only thing I've ever read that makes her seem like a human being.

Capote was a natural essayist: gossipy, insightful, honest, humane, a restless writer without much interest in conventions. My theory is that he only became a novelist because that's what writers were supposed to do. It's the same way now. Never mind that the contemporary novel is a zombie genre: if you want to be a real writer, you still have to write one. It's no accident that Capote called *In Cold Blood* a nonfiction *novel*. It was gambit for legitimacy, an attempt to make American readers, writers, and critics consider nonfiction as art. It mostly failed, but bless him for trying.

My book, *Son of a Gun*, was called a memoir. That's what the cover said. I thought of it as a hybrid, part memoir and part journalism and part biography, with a little historical and travel writing thrown in. But that's a pretentious and unwieldy thing to say, and my publisher said it would sell better if we called it a memoir, so I went along. By the time the book came out, and I was a newly minted memoirist,[159] that felt like a mistake. I didn't even like most memoirs, not the ones that read like fiction, and I didn't like fiction anymore, either, not novels or TV shows or movies. It seemed so formulaic and false, all that needless architecture, the rote

---

159. I still cringe whenever I'm called this.

banality of plots and arcs, grown-ups playing make believe. I wanted a kind of writing that took the best parts of different genres—journalism, fiction, critical writing, and memoir—and used them to build something better, a flexible form that didn't need so many arbitrary rules. I'd first been exposed to the literary essay in one of Charlie's classes, an American lit seminar I took in undergrad for which he assigned Joan Didion's *The White Album*.[160] I didn't know it at the time, but the blog posts I wrote for his Documentary Impulse class were essay exercises. Years later, I found myself returning to the form, rereading Baldwin and Didion, discovering contemporary essayists, teaching them in my classes. I wound up in the same place Capote did: writing essays.

It was a bad career move for both of us. Capote was still enough of a celebrity to make *Music for Chameleons* a commercial success, but the reviews were dismissive, and I've never met anyone else who's read it. He continued to work on *Answered Prayers*, or claimed to, but nobody expected him to finish, and I wonder if he did himself: his magnum opus had become a desperate myth, his last great success slipping over the horizon as the liquor and pills pulled him farther from shore. He signed the contract for his next nonfiction

---

160. Which deals at length with the Manson murders; Didion was also acquainted with Sharon Tate. Didion and Capote knew each other only slightly, according to Plimpton's oral history, although she did attend his funeral.

novel a few days before *In Cold Blood* came out. When he died, eighteen years later, it remained unfinished.[161]

The process of writing my next book was not so dramatic. My first book hadn't sold well, so nobody was in a hurry to publish my next one, and in truth I wasn't in a hurry to write another one, either. I wrote essays for a few years, including an early version of the third chapter of this book, and came up with a proposal for a collection, which Random House rejected. I couldn't sell my next two projects, either. My writing career was slipping away, and I needed to publish a book if I wanted to keep the professor job I'd spent a decade trying to get. So I made a deal with the devil, and pitched the one thing you can always sell in America: a book about a murder. Or even a book about a book about a murder.

·

Once we're done with *In Cold Blood*, my True Crime students take their midterm. Because it's a 100-level course full of freshmen and non-majors, people still relatively new to literary analysis, I give them an extra credit question at the end, a softball anyone can answer: *Do you care that Capote*

---

161. That didn't stop Random House from releasing it three years later as "the unfinished novel."

fictionalized parts of In Cold Blood*? Does it change your feelings about the book? Explain why or why not.*

Two-thirds of them say they don't care, that the degree of truth doesn't change their feelings about the book. It would be unprofessional to quote their answers, but their responses are insightful and smart. Many of the pro-Capote folks say they don't care about genres, or the distinction between fact and story, or that they don't expect stories, even true stories, to be completely true. Others say they only want a book to be entertaining. The pro-truth crowd is just as persuasive. They say it was wrong to change such important details, to lie to readers; they say Capote should have called it fiction, or at least not claimed every word of it was true.

Because the students have nothing much in common except age, it's tempting to read their responses as a consequence of their lifelong immersion in a quality and amount of media no other generation has experienced, all of it competing for their attention, approval, belief. But my class received the book more or less the same as the reading public of 1966, which also didn't care much that *In Cold Blood* was partly fabricated, if sales were any indication. Fifteen years ago, when I was a student reading the book for the first time, I didn't care much about the truth, either. The second time I read it, I still didn't: I was writing my own murder book by then, looking for techniques to steal. Now I'm teaching it for the fifth time, reading it for something like the tenth, and I know just about everything there is to know about the book. I can quote lines from memory, remember what page Perry's confession happens on, bore you to death with trivia—just ask my students. But I couldn't tell you how I feel about it, not in a sentence or two, not in this entire book. It depends on the context, the time of day, my mood at the moment. And the more I know about *In Cold Blood*, the more I learn about its author, the more my feelings about both change.

I would have liked Capote. I can tell from his work, the way others described him, the videos of him I watch online, pontificating on TV shows, playing for the camera in a way that makes you wonder how much he really hated fame. I admire his arrogance, his sand, the undeniable talent he wasn't afraid to acknowledge. At one point, a long time ago now, I thought we had things in common: we both grew up poor in backwaters, had itinerant childhoods and too many stepdads, took refuge in books and became writers. I thought I understood him in a way most people don't, because almost everyone who reads, reviews, or writes books in America comes from money. I admired the way he never fully left rural Alabama behind, held grudges and nurtured them, demanded admission to literary society even though he hated most of the people in it. We even had the same writerly wound, a dead mother, although his died of alcoholism—if she'd been murdered, like mine, *In Cold Blood* would be a different book. I've spent so much time now with Capote's work, reading and teaching it, carrying it with me, that his voice on the page feels like a friend's.

I don't like all of his work; his early fiction, especially, was slight, mannered, and overhyped. But his talent was immense. Everybody saw it, from the time he was a teenager. He said he was a genius, and he was right. He was also a professional. He produced and published work consistently for twenty years, stories, novels, essays, plays, screenplays, and whatever you want to call *In Cold Blood*. Capote called it many things, himself: a journalistic experiment, a new genre, a nonfiction novel, his greatest work. He was right about the latter, at least.

But like its hero's face, *In Cold Blood* changes when viewed from different angles. The book is an artistic marvel, and it affected me as a writer and thinker more than any other. On a craft level, as a piece of writing, a piece of art, it's almost perfect. As journalism, it's a sensationalized, unethical disaster. As an act of documentary, a historical account, it's appallingly biased. As a commercial product, a thing to be marketed and sold, it's been a unique success. As a new art form, the first nonfiction novel, it was mostly a failure. I admire *In Cold Blood*; I'm obsessed with *In Cold Blood*; I hate *In Cold Blood*. Most of all, I hate its legacy. The problem isn't that Capote fell in love with a murderer. The problem is that everyone else did, too.

In their answers to the extra credit question, none of my students object to Capote's most obvious fictionalization, making the murderer into a hero; whether or not they know it, they're used to that approach. They don't realize yet that Capote invented it. That's what the second half of the class is for.

.

We spend the rest of True Crime 101 tracking Capote's influence across the decades since *In Cold Blood*. Once true crime becomes popular, it's harder to choose texts. It might be interesting to read *The Executioner's Song* and discuss how Mailer's portrayal of Gary Gilmore mirrors Capote's of Perry Smith, but that book is a thousand pages long and would take the entire quarter. Most of the genre's tent poles are derivative, procedural pulp, and if this is the only literature course some of these students are ever going to take, I'm not going to make them read lawyer prose.

So we mix things up, throw in some new genres, problematize the concept of true crime. We read excerpts of *Beloved*, Toni Morrison's novel based on a historical murder, and an essay she wrote about her choice to write it as fiction. We read sections of Maggie Nelson's two books about her aunt's murder, *Jane* and *The Red Parts*—the first poetry,[162] the second a memoir—and talk about the ways they comment

---

162. Sort of: *Jane* is a hybrid of different forms and genres, and doesn't

on their own creation, and seem aware of the true crime tradition they operate in.[163]

Soon the class is sick of reading, so we skip ahead to the latest true crime boom, beginning with the text that started it: the podcast *Serial* by Sarah Koenig, which debuted in 2014, and is obviously a descendant of *In Cold Blood*. Both were released serially, probably as a nod to the tradition of radio dramas,[164] and we discuss other obvious similarities: both are about murder cases, tell their stories in innovative ways—mixing conventions of fiction and fact, relying heavily on dramatic irony—and mostly ignore the victims in favor of a deeply sympathetic look at the convicted killers.

From there, we move on to a strange new subgenre, true crime comedy. We listen to an episode of the *My Favorite Murder* podcast, created in 2016, and watch a Netflix show, *American Vandal*, which debuted the following year. Both offer a comic take on true crime, and they make the stories themselves the subject, turning a mirror toward a genre that's

claim a genre. You could argue that it's a book-length essay, and I probably would.

163. My teaching assistant suggested the Morrison and Nelson readings. Thanks, Tallon.

164. *Serial* makes this inspiration obvious, and Koenig has said in interviews that she was aware of the long tradition of the serial form. It's harder to say whether Capote's decision to serialize *In Cold Blood* was a conscious attempt to imitate radio dramas, but he did grow up in the era when they were most popular.

already perhaps too self-aware.[165] In *My Favorite Murder*, co-hosts Karen Kilgariff and Georgia Hardstuck discuss and analyze murder stories in a blithe and uncanny deadpan, as if they're talking about a sport or reality TV show. *American Vandal* takes it further, into a clever parody that uses the conventions of the genre—reenactments, an obsession with forensics, manipulating of time and space, withholding of information, blurring fact and fiction, even its own reflexive tendences—to mock true crime itself.

Despite spending over a month on *In Cold Blood*'s legacy, we don't come close to covering everything. That would take another class. This one enrolled well, so maybe that'll happen, and soon I'll be teaching True Crime 102, 201, 300, 400, a class on true crime film, a graduate course; maybe I'll call the latter the True Crime Impulse. I could trace the whole genealogy of *In Cold Blood*, all the way through my book, which by now has a complicated legacy of its own: Capote's book about a murder led me to write one of my own, which in turn led to this job, teaching murder stories, an expert in a field that shouldn't exist. That's one of the problems with *In Cold Blood*, reading it, teaching it, staring too long into its depths. You start to see yourself reflected darkly.

For example: I try to pretend, standing in front of

---

165. For much more on the reflexive and self-referential aspects of true crime, see Mark Seltzer's *True Crime: Observations on Violence and Modernity*, Routledge, 2007.

my students, talking about Perry Smith and the roots of murderer worship in America, that I haven't thought about the potential consequences of teaching a whole course about murder. Teaching *In Cold Blood* only inscribes it deeper in my mind. It also helps keep it alive for another generation of readers, creating more potential true crime fans, more worshippers in the cult.

·

Son of A Gun missed the latest true crime boom. It was released in 2013, a year before *Serial.* Had it come out two years later, it would probably have been marketed as a true crime memoir, another subgenre that has recently emerged. In a 2017 *Salon* article, Laura Miller described the phenomenon:

> The authors of these new true crime/memoir hybrids also put themselves at the center of the story to an extent that surpasses even the questing Sarah Koenig, producer and narrator of *Serial.* They spend less time describing how they tracked down facts or pored over forensic reports than they do scrutinizing their own feelings, turning them over and over like heirlooms.[166]

---

166. "True Crime Gets Pretty," August 15, 2017. https://slate.com/culture/

Miller goes on to critique writers of true crime memoirs for being self-absorbed, and for inserting their own interpretations into their books, in the form of thoughts and observations ascribed to real characters. Book critics have been lamenting the rise of personal nonfiction for decades, banging their gavels and calling for order, and Miller mostly recycles the same old critiques, based on the stale delusion that the goal of nonfiction writing is to reproduce some objective truth. As if truth and objectivity aren't foggy, relative notions; as if they don't reflect cultural agendas and vectors of power; as if any reasonable person could still believe, in a media landscape saturated by bias and propaganda, in a single, objective truth. As if anyone would want to read an objectively true story. As if it's possible to write one.

The most interesting part of Miller's article is when she offers Capote as a counterexample, a "scrupulous writer" who "resists the urge to fill in the blanks." Which is true, in the same selective sense as any true story, as long as you don't take into account Capote's ending, the killers' confessions, major aspects of their characters and motivations, multiple fabricated scenes, and many other parts of *In Cold Blood*. All these years later, after the book's truth has been repeatedly and publicly debunked—at a time when a simple Google

2017/08/the-true-crime-memoir-when-mfa-grads-and-literary-aspirants-write-true-crime.html This quote has been edited.

search will reveal abundant claims to the contrary—even some professional critics still somehow believe Capote's nonsense about it being "immaculately factual."

Miller is wrong about Capote not having inserted his subjective interpretations into *In Cold Blood*, but she's not alone. Capote convinced readers of his era and ours that his book was true, or at least not to care that it wasn't. And not just true, but *objective*. Even as he was running around calling *In Cold Blood* a "nonfiction novel"—often in the same interviews—he was constantly asserting it as journalism. A new and experimental kind, of course, but still journalism, still factual and unbiased, based on a quaint, arbitrary, and illogical interpretation of what truth means. I've read just about every word of nonfiction Capote wrote, and I can tell you what truth meant to him: not much. People only think *In Cold Blood* is objective because he told them to, and because he wrote it in third person, a literary parlor trick designed to fool readers into thinking he'd left himself out of the book.

I don't blame Capote for any of that; not anymore, at least. He knew how to sell books, and to tell people what they wanted to hear. If I'd had the chance, I might have let my publisher market my book as true crime. (It probably would've sold a lot better.) The shoe fit, in some ways: true crime has never been very true, and I changed all sorts of things in my book. Nothing that would get me sued; my publisher's lawyers made sure of that. (In a telling irony, they told me to change two characters' names, and leave out a couple of relevant details, so the legal read made my book *less* true.) But I rearranged events, consolidated characters, wrote long scenes and conversations based only on memory. Even the so-called facts got spun: some emphasized for effect, others left out. The sources, the facts and documents, police reports, confessions, photographs: those are static, non-narrative, anti-narrative. You have to arrange facts to suggest a relationship between them. Life doesn't have a plot, but stories do, and readers don't want facts, they want a *story*. In that sense, my students probably are a useful microcosm of American readers. Most of them don't care about the facts. They just want a story that *seems* true.

•

One gloomy weekend near the end of the class, I finally get around to watching *Cold Blooded: The Clutter Family Murders*, a 2017 miniseries directed by Joe Berlinger, a former acolyte of the Maysles brothers who went on to help define the genre of true crime documentaries. In an interview at the time of its release,[167] Berlinger said the project grew from

---

167. Green, Elon. "50 Years After 'In Cold Blood,' a New Look at the Clutter Family Murders." *MEL Magazine*, November 17, 2017. Available here: https://medium.com/mel-magazine/50-years-after-in-cold-blood-a-new-look-at-the-clutter-family-murders-5f702cdb3d4b.

his obsession with *In Cold Blood*, which he was assigned in high school and has reread since. He says the book shaped his fascination with crime, and the kind of filmmaker he became. Sounds familiar.

Berlinger discusses the evolution of documentary since the Maysles, whose direct cinema philosophy—like Capote's theory of the nonfiction novel—believed in mimesis. "That was the main tenet of the direct cinema philosophy," Berlinger says. "That you're capturing an objective reality." But Berlinger doesn't believe any media is objective, and calls filmmaking *"extremely* subjective."[168] He says it can be truthful, and should be, but distinguishes between the notions of objectivity and truth by offering the same justification many memoirists do: that his films try to capture "the emotional truth of a situation, of the human condition."

Berlinger uses his first film, *Brother's Keeper*, as an example. He codirected the 1992 documentary about a murder in rural New York, and says he made creative decisions that drew on fictional forms: namely, he imposed a dramatic structure, and added an original musical score. "It was a synthesis of documentary and narrative technique," he says. "And where did that come from? My obsession with Capote."

Berlinger's wrangling with *In Cold Blood* led him to the

---

168. Italics his.

same conclusion mine did. "Books and movies about the Clutter murders have all been at the expense of the victims of the family members," he says, extending that criticism to himself and the whole genre: "What happens in true crime is we make literary heroes out of the criminals, at the expense of the family members and victims." *Cold Blooded* claims, somewhat inaccurately,[169] that it includes the first public statements from the surviving members of the Clutter family since the murders. But Berlinger goes well beyond interviewing them: his film seems like a corrective, a retelling of Capote's story with an emphasis on the victims, an act of restorative justice.

Like *In Cold Blood*, Berlinger's documentary begins with Holcomb, and the Clutters themselves. He interviews their friends and relatives, and includes family photographs and the only known video footage of Herb and Bonnie, brief and haunting black-and-white clips of them working on River Valley Farm, shot in 1952 for a CBS News report. The images of them on my TV screen look faltering and unreal, like

---

169. As Green points out, family members—including the surviving daughters—have spoken to reporters before. (Technically, Bonnie Clutter's brother does so in *In Cold Blood*, shortly after the murders.) And Diana Edwards, whom Berlinger interviews in the film, published the aforementioned essay. But *Cold Blooded* does present many previously unseen materials from the family, including parts of their scrapbook, as well as a number of interviews with relatives and close friends of the Clutters, including Bobby Rupp.

memories, like ghosts. Bonnie does laundry; Herb drives a tractor. He talks about the economics of farming; she remains silent, mostly offscreen. The great lie of documentary: it seems so objective, so real, as if that's who they really were, as if it couldn't have been any other way. It takes me back to Charlie's class, all those years ago, discussing Sebald, memory, simulacra, the tyranny of the image.

Cold Blooded borrows the four-part structure of Capote's book: the crime, investigation, trial, and execution.[170] It tells essentially the same story Capote did, in the same order, and Berlinger uses interviews and sources directly, with no voiceover, the filmic equivalent of Capote's objective third person, which gave the illusion that there was no narrator shaping *In Cold Blood*. Like Capote, Berlinger has an obvious bias, and uses fictional techniques, reenactments and unrelated footage, a score that provides emotional cues. But the differences are obvious early on: *Cold Blooded* focuses more on the Clutters[171] and the community, around them, dramatically less on the killers. The sections about the

---

170. More or less: Berlinger's film is more reflexive, incorporating the story of Capote's book, and also devotes significant time to the fifty years since its release, its legacy and impact. It's also worth noting that *Cold Blooded* may have originally aired on Sundance in two parts—Green's interview says as much—although it's split into four parts on Amazon Video, where I watched it.

171. To the point of including crime-scene photos of their bodies, a startling and arguably exploitative choice.

murderers focus more on Hickock than Smith. I wind up binge-watching the entire series in a day, and it reads like a revision of *In Cold Blood*, the story of the Clutter murders told by someone who wasn't in love with Perry Smith.

The last section of *Cold Blooded* diverges to discuss the movie adaptation of *In Cold Blood*, and a few eerie parallels between the movie and real life. The film was shot on location, and many of the spectators who showed up at the courthouse to see it being filmed had also been there the day Dewey walked the killers up the steps; seven of the original jurors even reprised their roles in the movie. Capote's vision defined the movie almost as much as it did the book: he had input on directors and casting, and Berlinger includes clips of him on set outside the Clutter house. Principals from the movie discuss the fraught experience of shooting on location, reenacting the murders in the rooms where they occurred. The actors who played Nancy Clutter and Dick Hickock say they had bad dreams for years afterward; the former, Brenda Currin, calls them "guilt-based nightmares," and says that after watching the film for the first time, she wanted to walk out into traffic. "It was really authentic," said Quincy Jones, who wrote the movie's score.[172] "It smelled like the situation. It felt like the situation." Robert Blake, the relative unknown who played Perry Smith, doesn't appear in *Cold Blooded* much, but Berlinger includes a

---

172. His score was nominated for an Academy Award.

video clip in which Blake erupts when an interviewer asks if he thinks the film glorifies the killers. He claims his only job was to show what really happened: "I don't want a fiction," Blake says. He may have taken the truth too far: thirty years later, he was accused of murdering his wife, and acquitted in a high-profile trial newspapers called "grist for a true-life pulp novel."[173]

Berlinger portrays *In Cold Blood* not only as a genre-defining sensation, but as a curse that hung over everyone involved. The sections of the film about Capote's subsequent self-destruction trod a worn path, the alcohol and drugs, his oft-repeated quote about how writing the book had scraped him to the marrow, the public antics and embarrassments, Clarke claiming that his friend never survived *In Cold Blood*. The only part that's new to me is a clip from an interview with Capote[174] where he is asked about the Clutter family's reaction to his portrayal of Bonnie. Capote seems aggrieved by the question, and deflects it by mentioning a letter the family's minister had sent to a newspaper, saying they were unhappy with it. He claimed that was all he knew about the subject.

Berlinger's documentary, unlike any other account of the Clutter killings I've ever seen, acknowledges what *In*

---

173. Leduff, Charlie. "Actor's Trial, Complete With Pulp Novel Characters, Draws to a Close." *New York Times*, March 5, 2005, https://www.nytimes.com/2005/03/05/us/actors-trial-complete-with-pulp-novel-characters-draws-to-a-close.html.

174. The provenance of the clip isn't mentioned in the film, but it appears at approximately 22:20 of episode 4.

Cold Blood has done to the family and the community, and gives space for them to respond. It shows a list the surviving Clutter daughters made after reading the book's first installment in *The New Yorker* of forty-five inaccuracies in that section alone, most relating to its portrayal of their mother. In an onscreen interview, Diana Selsor Edwards reads the line from her editorial about the Clutters being cardboard figures, and talks about the reverberations of a murder like that, how it affects the whole community, as well as multiple generations. A Clutter granddaughter who refuses to show her face onscreen laments that the story just won't go away, and says she resents the reduction of her relatives to victims. "They weren't just murdered," she says. "They were wonderful people." Near the end, Berlinger includes a quiet, devastating moment with Bobby Rupp, Nancy's boyfriend, the last person to see the family alive. I stop the movie, stare at his face, and try to remember my trip with Bonnie to Holcomb, the old man who spit in the dirt when I said I liked the book. I can't tell if it was him. Still, it makes me wish I'd never gone to see the house.

Maybe it's a testament to Berlinger's documentary, or maybe it's just my own bias, but as I watched *Cold Blooded*, I sympathized with the Clutters, their relatives, the people of Holcomb. Like them, I also wish *In Cold Blood* would go away, but know it won't. Not for them, not for me, not for any of us. It's already spread too far, been around too long, and the genre it inspired has propagated like kudzu across Capote's native Alabama.

Cold Blooded briefly mentions other aspects of the book's legacy, the factual issues, the Walker murder investigation and disinterment of the killers, the public's enduring fascination with Smith and Hickock, and the genre it created, itself a curse of sorts. "This book is where we got the genre of true crime," says Corbin Crable, a Kansas journalist and professor. "But at what cost?"[175] Berlinger seems to be saying what I've come to believe, after reading and rereading the book for all these years: *In Cold Blood* is a ghost haunting every murder story since it was published, a dark mirror reflecting our worst impulses, the beginning of our love affair with killers.

•

In Cold Blood is not like other books. It gets inside you, nests, infects. For instance, the book is full of dreams—all of Capote's work is—Perry Smith's big heroic bird, the Clutters appearing to the Deweys in their sleep.[176] I don't dream much, never have,

---

175. Coincidentally, Crable was committing a crime when Berlinger interviewed him: not long after, he was fired from the college where he worked for misappropriating funds.

176. The worst writing in the book is a dream sequence: Dewey walks into a cafe in Garden City and sees Herb Clutter having lunch with his murderers. When he tries to shoot them, the room becomes a nearby swimming pool, then a graveyard, Valley View, where he takes refuge behind his father's

but a certain paranoia comes to me sometimes, when I'm awake, late at night, unable to sleep, especially on nights like that one long ago, clear and windy, the moon bright in the sky. I live in a midcentury ranch near the edge of a small town surrounded by farms, with a wife named Bonnie and a rambunctious boy and a dog who's afraid of guns. I try not to think too much about what would happen if I heard footsteps in the hall, saw a flashlight carve the darkness, two men at my bedroom door. What Herb must have felt, kneeling on a box in his own basement. Kenyon lying on the couch, staring down a barrel. Nancy begging for mercy, turning her head. Bonnie hearing boots at the door and saying a prayer. My mother, all those years later, doing the same. That's what they've become, now that they've been dead so long. They're not even people anymore, just a point someone's always trying to make. An ending for a story—like Capote's, and like this one—that isn't even theirs.

·

Write a book about a murder and you'll get some strange correspondence. For me, it was mostly emails and social media messages, a few handwritten letters. Some were from fellow family members of murder victims who read my book

---

gravestone as Smith and Hickock stand astride the Clutter grave, cackling. Dewey shoots them, they disappear, and he wakes up.

and wanted to respond, often by telling me their own stories of loved ones snatched and erased by violence. Some were from people who knew my mother long ago. Occasionally, I'll hear from someone who thinks the story of my mother's death might make a good televsion show.

The most persistent are representatives of a channel called Investigation Discovery. I make a point of avoiding true crime unless I'm teaching it, so I had never heard of Investigation Discovery, and I had some questions, including why its name was two vague, redundant nouns. So I searched the internet, as one does, and made a discovery of my own: the channel is a case study in true crime. It originated in 2008, as a rebranding of an existing channel under the Discovery umbrella, which had twice failed under different names and foci: first as a channel devoted to ancient cultures, then as a short-lived collaboration with the *New York Times*. When the latter show folded, the network's executives tried an unprecedented gambit by turning it into the first TV channel devoted entirely to true crime.

It worked: Discovery Investigation was a runaway hit. The channel's revenues doubled over the next four years. By 2015, it was the highest-rated cable network among women between the ages of twenty-five to fifty-four, including celebrity fans like Lady Gaga and Serena Williams.[177]

---

177. See Battaglio, Stephen. "Investigation Discovery Becomes Top Cable

Investigation Discovery was so successful that Oxygen, a rival network previously devoted to programming for women, soon followed suit, switching to 24/7 true crime, a change less drastic than it might sound: despite the genre's fetish for female victims, the audience for true crime is mostly women, for reasons nobody has satisfactorily answered, despite frequent media speculation.[178]

To fill all that airtime, true crime channels have to create hundreds of hours of original programming every year. That's a lot of murders. And one of the paradoxes of the latest true crime boom is that as America's fascination with murder stories has skyrocketed, its murder rate has fallen. Fewer murders happen in America now than at any point since *In Cold Blood*.[179] Even fewer fit the formula Capote created for the true crime genre, of strangers committing

Channel for Women with True Crime All the Time." *Los Angeles Times*, January 5, 2016. https://www.latimes.com/entertainment/envelope/cotown/la-et-ct-investigation-discovery-20160105-story.html.

178. A University of Illinois study documented the true crime gender divide. See Yates, Diana, "Women, More than Men, Choose True Crime Over Other Violent Nonfiction." University of Illinois News Bureau, February 15, 2010. https://news.illinois.edu/view/6367/205718 In recent years, the *New York Times*, *CBS News*, *The Atlantic*, and the *Hairpin*, among others, have speculated about the reasons behind it.

179. The relationship between true crime and crime itself is too complicated and convoluted to cover here in any depth, but the publication of *In Cold Blood* coincided with a huge spike in the American murder rate, which doubled between 1966 and 1980, remained high until the early 1990s, and has been steadily declining since, despite a modest rise in the last few years, as of this writing.

seemingly motiveless crimes that suggest something about our culture. True crime channels have had to expand their definition of the genre, making shows about crimes that once would have seemed too mundane, the most common kinds of actual murders: crimes of passion, people killing people they know. In that sense, true crime has gotten truer, but it seems like a cynical innovation: now that they've run out of sensational murders, the genre's content creators have resorted to making any old murder seem sensational. That's where I come in.

The first emails from Investigation Discovery were formal and polite. A British gentleman said he'd come across my mother's story while researching a new true crime series, what he assured me was "serious documentary." We arranged a time to talk, and he called from London and spoke with me for quite some time, explaining his show and its approach. He told me it was his third TV series, and it wasn't the sort of sensationalized true crime I might be used to. His show was much more respectful and victim-centered, and he used home videos whenever possible, not dramatic recreations. He seemed to be avoiding saying the name of the show, so I asked him directly. It was called *American Monster*. So much for being victim-centered.

He said he'd heard about my mother—he mentioned my book, although I got the sense he hadn't read it—and was interested in possibly making an episode about her. I asked what he wanted from me. He said I could participate, but didn't have to. He mostly seemed to want family photos, home videos, the kind of things we talk about in True Crime 101 as truth claims, reminders to the viewer: *this is real.* The producer said he couldn't pay me for my participation, beyond a small honorarium—that would be unethical— but he would pay for the rights to any home videos I could provide, possibly thousands of dollars, depending on the amount. And, of course, he'd make sure to mention my book on the show. He mentioned the 1.7 million viewers per episode, and how popular the show was among women twenty-five to fifty-four, the same demographic who buys the most books.

I'd like to say I told him to go fuck himself. But it didn't seem like an unreasonable request, and I had no right to be outraged by someone else asking to turn my mother's death into a product when I'd done the same thing; if I hadn't written *Son of A Gun*, we would've never had that conversation. And he seemed like a decent enough guy: a little corporate, maybe, more of a businessman than an artist, but then again, I was the one teaching a true crime class. But I know better by now than to trust anyone who made true crime, so I said I'd have to think about it.

I asked Bonnie what she thought. She said it seemed like a bad idea, unless I wanted to write about it. Did I? Like most writing ideas, it sounded good at first—I briefly imagined the rave reviews about my trenchant meditation on the nature of truth—but got worse the more I thought about it. Writing about someone making a TV show based on my writing would be too reflexive, too self-involved, too far up its own ass, even for a memorist. But I still couldn't make up my mind. Even if I wanted to participate, I wasn't sure how much home video we had.

I went through what was left of my mother, the fragments I'd collected in the half of my life since her death. It wasn't not much, a couple of cardboard boxes on a shelf in my office closet, stored next to unopened boxes of my book about her. Most of it was her military relics, photographs, and other personal effects, some still in evidence bags. My mother liked photography, was always buying camcorders and filming our Christmases, so I found a fair amount of video of her, of my family, the life that ended when she died. I'd had some of it digitized when I was writing about her, and used it in my book as source material, a way to include her more directly, a truth claim. But I got to select what went in, and I controlled the description and arrangement of the clips themselves; in somebody else's hands, they might tell another story. I hadn't watched the videos since I was writing the book, years ago, in what already seemed like another life. Seeing my mother onscreen did its work, reminding me in some simulacric, Sebaldian way of what had been lost, and all the ways my portrayal of her was wrong or insufficient.

I had gotten the impression there would be no show without these videos. It wasn't going to be a Capote-and-the-Clutter-family scenario, where they would tell the story either way: too much time had passed, and these TV producers didn't have years to spend investigating. They weren't trying to invent a new art form; they just needed grist for the mill.

I thought of my mother's few surviving friends and relatives, and how they'd feel if they turned on the TV one day and saw her onscreen. I tried to imagine how she would feel, but writing *Son of A Gun* had taught me that I couldn't. Mom was kind of like Capote: a tiny terror, tough and savvy, nobody's fool. She might have told me to take the money,[180] to think about my career: maybe I could parlay it into more publicity, pitch related articles at high-profile media outlets, help sell one of my other books nobody wanted.

That's what Capote would have done. He loved the camera, the spotlight, the opportunity for controversy. All publicity was good publicity to Capote, no matter who it hurt, even—perhaps especially—if it was himself. His true crime book made him an icon, the most famous writer in the world, a household name. But he lost control of his own life, and became the subject of a story other people told: his decline, his death, his legacy.

---

180. I want to say it was $1500, but can't remember for sure.

I said no. Maybe I'd read too much about the Clutters, their family and friends and neighbors, what they went through. Maybe I still felt guilty for going to Holcomb to gawk at their trauma. Or maybe I just knew too much about true crime, enough to know better when they said they wanted to make a different kind of true crime, one that respected the victims, their families, their community. The same thing Capote had said, in the beginning.

Acknowledgments

I would like to gratefully acknowledge the scholars, writers, filmmakers, and critics whose work was consulted for this book. The following were especially important to this project: Ralph F. Voss' *Truman Capote and the Legacy of In Cold Blood*; Gerald Clarke's *Capote*; George Plimpton's *Truman Capote: In Which Various Friends, Enemies, Acquaintances, and Detractors Recall His Turbulent Career*; Harold Schechter's *True Crime: An American Anthology*; Jean Murley's *True Crime: 20th-Century Murder and American Popular Culture*; Michael Renov's "Toward a Poetics of Documentary"; Bill Nichols' *Representing Reality*; Joe Berlinger's TV series *Cold Blooded: The Clutter Family Murders*; and Capote's nonfiction, especially *Music for Chameleons*, *Portraits and Observations: The Essays of Truman Capote*, and, of course, *In Cold Blood*.

Parts of this book first appeared as an essay in *Tin House*, which was included in the Pushcart Prize anthology. I'm grateful to both for giving it an audience, and to the editors at Tin House, whose keen eyes made the piece better, especially Emma Komlos-Hrobsky. My deepest thanks to Robert Lasner and Ig Publishing, who took a chance on this book when it was an idea in an email from a stranger; I'm honored to be a part of the Bookmarked series.

Thanks also to the many friends, colleagues, and fellow writers whose advice, feedback, and conversation helped during the writing process, especially Charlie Bertsch, Laurel Dixon, George Estreich, Elena Passarello, and David Turkel. Tallon Kennedy was the TA for the true crime class I write about in Part 4, and our co-teaching and conversations helped inform this project in various ways. I'm also grateful to my students, who have taught me a lot about true crime.

And thanks to Bonnie and Arlo, for putting up with me while I was writing this, and for bringing so much joy into my life.